WITHDRAWN
UTSA Libraries

SIDNEY LUMET

Sidney
LUMET

*a guide to
references and resources*

*A
Reference
Publication
in
Film*

Ronald Gottesman
Editor

Sidney LUMET

a guide to references and resources

STEPHEN E. BOWLES

G.K. HALL & CO.
70 LINCOLN STREET, BOSTON, MASS.

Distributed in United Kingdom and Europe
by George Prior Associated Publishers Ltd.
37–41 Bedford Row
London WC1R 4JH, England

LIBRARY
The University of Texas
At San Antonio

Copyright © 1979 by

Library of Congress Cataloging in Publication Data

Bowles, Stephen E   1943-
   Sidney Lumet, a guide to references & resources.

   (A Reference publication in film)
   Includes indexes.
   1. Lumet, Sidney, 1924-   2. Moving-picture producers and directors—United States—Biography. 3. Moving-picture plays—History and criticism. I. Title. II. Series.
PN1998. A3L883   791.43'0233'0924   [B]   79-475
ISBN 0-8161-7938-7

This publication is printed on permanent/durable acid-free paper
MANUFACTURED IN THE UNITED STATES OF AMERICA

For Ann, with love.

Contents

Preface xi
Acknowledgments xiii
Biographical Background 1
Critical Survey of Oeuvre 35
The Films: Synopses, Credits, and Notes 63
Annotated Guide to Writings about Lumet 115
List of Performances and Writings (and Other
    Film-related Activities) 123
Reviews and References 129
Distributors of Lumet's Films 143
Title Index 149
Name Index 151

Preface

It is surprising how comparatively few critical studies have been done on Sidney Lumet. Like many projects, the writing of this book began as a challenge — to fill an important scholarly gap — and turned into a labor of love — to satisfy a probing curiosity.

Since Lumet's career really began at the age of four, a liberal amount of space has been devoted to profiling his life. Most everything, it seems in retrospect, that Lumet has attempted since the age of four has a direct bearing on his career as a film director. One of Lumet's strengths is his ability to look at his work and himself, and to criticize both. He has admitted, for example, that *That Kind of Woman* is "pretty crummy" and agreed that *Long Day's Journey into Night* is "nearly perfect."

In the text of this book, therefore, I have attempted to present (1) a personality portrait of Lumet, (2) a brief accounting of his various careers, and (3) an overview of his films. Inserted into this account of his life and films are a generous number of comments both by and about Lumet, commenting on his career at period points.

Although Sidney Lumet is always a director before he is a philosopher, he has repeatedly emphasized a consistency of thought that strongly bears upon his life and work. It is worth recounting a few of these statements here.

Lumet's motto:
  "If you're a director, direct!"
About motion pictures:
  "It is the last and only medium in which it is possible to tell a story of conscience, outside the printed word."
  "My only criterion for what constitutes a film is, Does the film tell *that* story better, and more revealingly, and more movingly than any other medium can?"
About filmmaking:
  "If you care about your work, every frame matters."
About directing:
  "There's no great secret about directing. The job is to get the best out of

every element of the production. So the better the elements are, hopefully the results are going to be that much fuller."

About his method:

"I don't have any hard and fast rules."

About actors:

"I think actors are the best people in the world."

"Good work in movies involves personal exposure, personal risks, showing how you feel about something. The actor is infinitely more exposed than anyone else, and he's exposed at the very moment of creativity. Actors are the infantry, the ones in the line of fire."

About the camera:

"The camera becomes *another* leading actor. . . . You have to cast your camera the way you cast an actor."

About his aesthetic:

"For me, photographing a human face that is *saying* something profound is as much cinema as a chariot race."

"I spend an awful lot of time on them [close-ups] because it's what interests me most."

About his career:

"You have your hot flashes, your cold flashes; it's the body of work that counts."

About reality:

"I'm not one to be cool about a hit, having had so many flops. I know the market place, and I know you need hits to survive in it."

About survival:

"I survive because of an insane inner tempo. My energy seldom fails me."

About his life:

"I'm a happy man because I'm doing what I want to do."

Acknowledgments

I would like to thank both Mr. Lumet for his generous cooperation and the British Film Institute for graciously opening their research facilities to me. Thanks are also due to Mr. Larry Estes of Films, Incorporated, to Swank Films, Budget Films, Warner Brothers and United Artists for providing prints from their collections to screen for this project.

Special thanks, beyond a mere acknowledgement, must be extended to Pam Kimball and Ann Walters for their very important research contributions. Without Pam and Ann, it is unlikely that the book would have been published.

Biographical Background

Sidney Lumet is neither part of the "old guard" of film directors from the thirties and forties nor of the new "film school" directors of the seventies. He has worked as a professional in radio, theatre, television and films. He is hardly the flamboyant and conspicuous director that many people expect an internationally respected filmmaker to be. He rarely gives interviews and is never seen on celebrity talk shows. Lumet is usually too preoccupied in a current project to be distracted by such ego-feeding banalities.

Lumet is typically described as wearing a denim shirt, faded dungarees, and perhaps a wind-breaker and sneakers. John Crosby once referred to him as "a tiny leprechaun";[1]* Elizabeth Trotta characterized him as "a small man in faded denim, [who] compensated for his lack of height with cushion-soled shoes";[2] Guy Flatley observed the "short, mild-mannered man . . . [who] looks almost elfin" [51]; London-based reporter Stephen Watts remarked that a "small whirlwind called Sidney Lumet has just swept through here";[3] and Gene Moskowitz called him "small, spectacled, and extremely youthful and talkative in a fast, piercing way" [27]. Everyone who knows him seems overwhelmed by the robust vitality and charisma emanating from the small (5'-7") frame.

From the beginning of his career, Lumet has typically been characterized by four distinct and consistent qualities: his respect for actors, his reliability as a director, his boundless energy, and his contempt for Hollywood.

Of all the tributes accorded to Lumet over the years, probably the best known is his great fondness for and skill with performers. "I love actors" is probably his most frequently quoted expression. Despite the criticisms that have been levelled against him, he is consistently praised for his consummate ability to draw powerful acting performances from his casts.

In a chapter he contributed to the anthology *Movie People*, Lumet evaluates his relationship with actors. "I work well with actors, and I know I have

---

*The numbers in brackets following a quotation refer to the entry numbers corresponding to the bibliographical citations in Sections IV and V. Superior numbers refer to notes at the end of each chapter. Quotations without any reference numbers indicate personal statements made by Lumet to the author.

gotten the reputation of being an 'actor's director.' I think that the primary reason for this is that, having been an actor myself, I do not have the normal director's contempt for the actor, the Hitchcockian attitude that 'they're all children.' . . . As for myself, I understand the critical point about actors: their baring of selves, their personal revelation. And that is something I respect, will be gentle with, will never violate. . . . It is the respect for their personal revelations, I think, that made those actors want to work with me in the first place" [82]. In a statement quoted in *Action*, Lumet reinforces his convictions: "I'm not an actor-hating director. I don't use actors as puppets. Next to stand-up nightclub comics, actors are the guttiest people in the world."[4] And from his own memories, Lumet refers to "The moments Marlon Brando gave me in *The Fugitive Kind*, or Sean Connery in *The Hill* or Kate Hepburn in *Journey* — I felt lucky just to be alive at the same time as she is — or Mason or Fonda or dozens of others I have worked with. Those moments I could not get from any other source but the real actor. That's why I love them."[5] And, as a crowning tribute, he commented to Rex Reed, "One of the joys of my life is I never had an actor who didn't want to come back for a second time. I get to actors."[6]

Lumet's affection and compassion for actors is reciprocated by the actors' love for him. Sean Connery, who has appeared in three Lumet films, has publicly called him "one of my favorite directors."[7] Simone Signoret, who has been in two of his films, dubbed him "a little bull. . . . He has fantastic energy, he's optimistic, he's nice, he loves actors."[8] Robert Hooks, in an interview with Rex Reed during the filming of *Last of the Mobile Hot-Shots* in Louisiana, said, "Man, I thought I'd never come back down here again [after making *Hurry Sundown*], but I just couldn't turn down a chance to work with Sidney."[9] Working on the same film, James Coburn told Reed, "Sidney is the only director I've ever worked with who makes me feel I'm working toward a totality instead of a piece of nothing. . . . On this film, I feel like I'm just learning what the work is all about."[10] On the set of *Bye, Bye Braverman*, George Segal told reporters, "I've worked with a lot of directors but I have to say he's fantastic. . . . You can't help but enjoy working with him."[11] Dirk Bogarde once said, "If Lumet calls me up, I will do anything he wants me to do." (Bogarde's tribute is especially impressive, if ironic, since he has never appeared in a Lumet film.)

Certainly as strong as his reputation with actors is Lumet's reputation as a "reliable" director. With all the Hollywood horror stories about escalating budgets and extended shooting schedules, Lumet has consistently made his films with a rare combination of economy and speed. A classic example of this was *Serpico*, which Lumet took over only a few weeks before shooting was to begin. Despite having more than a hundred different location shots around New York and more than a hundred speaking parts, the film was completed in ten weeks — a remarkable four days *ahead* of schedule. "The trick," according to Lumet, "is to be controlled. Don't go wild. Be honest. If you think the film will cost 1.2 million, bring it in for 1.2 million; don't go 100,000 over budget."[12]

How does he manage to work so fast with such efficiency? "Sidney has the ability to get everybody together. . . . [He] is a tremendously organized director," remarks Roger Rothstein, the associate producer of *Serpico* [52]. "Fast? Hell, no," Lumet claimed while filming *Bye, Bye Braverman*. "We're totally organized and rehearsed. This is a seven week schedule . . . and we intend to keep it. Why not?"[13]

Practically everyone testifies to the contagious and tireless energy that Lumet radiates. Rarely in the two decades he's been directing feature films has he not been working on a project, usually preparing the next one while editing the previous one while shooting the current one. "I guess it's my metabolism," he once speculated. "I never walk down a hall, I bound down a hall. And when I make a movie, I work fast."[14] After finishing *The Group*, for example, Lumet told London interviewer Stephen Watts, "I'd die of boredom on a long picture. Anyhow, my natural level of energy and concentration is suited to this pace. But remember, I spend a lot of time on preparation and I always rehearse. Once I know exactly what I'm going to do, I get on with it."[15]

For those who accuse him of making too many films too fast, Lumet replies, "Nonsense. I turn them in on time and that gives me time to do more. These directors who set out to turn every movie into a masterpiece are selling themselves short. . . . My training in live TV taught me to literally carry around eight shows a week in my head for two years. Now I can't work on one project without another in the planning stage. . . . The reason most directors go over budget and take so long is they don't know what they want. I know actors and I know the camera. That's why my movies are well-acted and well-photographed."[16]

The fourth, and in many ways the most historically significant, characteristic that has remained with Lumet from the beginning of his career is his public disdain for "Hollywood." Deliberately selecting material that would permit him to work on locations outside Hollywood, Lumet helped establish New York City as a major production center long before it became fashionable. Seventeen of Lumet's twenty-five features were based and shot in New York. Six others were made in Europe and one was shot in the South.

His dislike for Hollywood has been voiced on numerous occasions. Discussing his location filming (in Rome) for *The Appointment*, he commented, "Filming in Hollywood is like filming in a company town. That's all that goes on there, filming, there is no life outside filming. I respect somebody else's bag, and obviously it works for other people. But for me Hollywood isn't organic, it's a place not fit for human habitation. When you work there, you work in isolation. I hate being separated from all other life. . . . In New York there is so much life — other life, not movie life — going on around you that even if you don't have time to read the paper you can't escape being aware of the world out there."[17]

Owen Roizman, three-time Academy Award nominee for his cinematography (including *Network*), perhaps revealed most about Sidney Lumet. "Sidney is the kind of guy who is pretty hard not to get along with. He's terrific. He knows his stuff and he's so professional and so well-prepared that I can't say enough for him. He's great fun and he controls everybody so well. Working with him is really a pleasure" [55].

Sidney Lumet was born in Philadelphia on June 25, 1924. Of two children, he was the only son of Baruch and Eugenia (Wermus) Lumet. Baruch Lumet had been trained as an actor in Poland at the Warsaw Academy of Dramatic and Musical Arts, where he made his acting debut in 1918. After a brief period in London, the Lumets immigrated to the United States, where, in 1926, the elder Lumet became associated with Maurice Schwartz's acting troupe at the Yiddish Art Theatre in New York City. After acting experience both on and off Broadway, Baruch Lumet toured the United States, Canada and Mexico with his own one-man show ("Monotheatre Varieties") from 1939 through 1946. On television he appeared in teleplays on *Studio One, Kraft Television Theatre,* and *Playhouse 90,* and in episodes of *The Untouchables, The Detectives, Alfred Hitchcock Presents, The Dick Powell Theatre, The Eleventh Hour,* and *Arrest and Trial.* In films he has had minor roles in *One Third of a Nation* (1939), *Killer Shrews* (1959), *Is This for Me?* (1961), *The Interns* (1962), and *Adventures of a Young Man* (1962), as well as several parts in his son's films, most notably as the cantankerous Mendel in *The Pawnbroker* (1965) and the kindly Mr. Schneider in *The Group* (1966). In addition to Baruch Lumet's other varied talents, he was director of the Dallas Institute of Performing Arts from 1953 to 1960 and wrote and starred in the 1975 play *Autumn Fever.*

Although born in Philadelphia, Sidney Lumet must be considered a product of New York's lower East Side, where he has lived and worked since the age of two. He began acting at five and has been acting or directing ever since.

Lumet made his acting debut with his father in a 1928 production at the Yiddish Theatre. At that time, the Yiddish Theatre, composed primarily of European refugees who had come to the United States, was flourishing in New York (12 separate companies on 40-week seasons). The theatrical activity specialized in the grand old style of operatic productions, which was, even then, becoming passé. Also in that year, Lumet got his first introduction to radio, since his father was serving as writer-director-actor in a series of radio dramas emanating from a small Yiddish station in Brooklyn. One of the more famous radio programs of the late twenties and through the thirties, in which Lumet had a small role, was a "children's drama" called

The Adventures of Helen and Mary (later re-titled *Let's Pretend*). It became known as "radio's outstanding children's theatre," delighting youngsters with stories of ghosts, witches, princes, leprechauns, speaking animals and so on.

The young Lumet's success and interest in acting kept him busy for the next five years, as he continued to play children's roles in radio and on the Yiddish stage. Years later, Lumet reflected back on this period, "Acting was an economic necessity in our family during the depression, and for two years — 1931 and 1932 — I was on a weekly WEVD radio show, in Yiddish, called *The Rabbi from Brownsville*. My father wrote and directed the show and acted the leading man and the grandfather. My mother was the leading lady, and I played the son. All together, our weekly salary came to $35."[18]

At the age of eleven, the youthful Lumet made his Broadway debut (October 28, 1935) at the Belasco Theater, playing one of the tough New York City Dead End Kids in Sidney Kingsley's *Dead End*. The play signalled what, arguably, was the height of realism in the theatre, uncompromisingly moving between brutality and gentleness. Reminiscing some forty years later, Lumet foundly recalls, "I was 11 at the time and at the time had already been in eight Jewish plays. But since I was always small for my age, I couldn't play one of the Dead End Kids. So Sidney [Kingsley], who adored me, wrote a special bit into the play for me."[19]* Both the play and the period were to have a profound effect on Lumet's future development. "That was the period of realistic theatre in America," he recalls in a 1974 interview. "I guess the directing style I have now stemmed from that."[20]

An important event for the young actor occurred when he was given the role of the youthful Jesus in Max Reinhardt's version of *The Eternal Road*. One of the stars of the production was the famous Lotte Lenya,* wife of the show's composer, Kurt Weill. Also in the cast was his father, who played the Third Pious Man. The play opened on January 7, 1937, and Lumet, playing one of the leading parts, won the recognition of several critics and a succession of Broadway performances.

Over the next few years, Lumet had roles in eight major Broadway productions (several of which were unsuccessful). He played Stanley in *Sunup to Sundown*, directed by Joseph Losey, at the Hudson Theatre; Mickey in *Schoolhouse on the Lot* at the Ritz; Johnny in William Saroyan's *My Heart's in the Highlands*; Leo in *Christmas Eve* at the Henry Miller Theatre; Hymie Tashman in *Morning Star* at the Longacre Theatre; a juvenile replacement in

---

*As a sort of tribute to his long friendship with Kingsley, Lumet filmed the party sequence in *Serpico* in Kingsley's Fifth Avenue loft.

*In fond remembrance of Ms. Lenya, Lumet used her as a key character in *The Appointment*.

George Washington Slept Here; Joshua, the young Jesus, in *Journey to Jerusalem* at the National Theatre; and Willie Berg, a young hoodlum, in *Brooklyn U.S.A.* at the Forrest.

Lumet had his introduction to the movie business in 1939 when the play *One Third of a Nation* was filmed as it was running simultaneously on the stage. Dudley Murphy, producer of both the play and the film, was one of the first to attempt filmmaking in New York at a time when location shooting was quite rare. "My idea," he announced at the time, "is to produce a play a year on Broadway. Then, concurrently with the run of the Broadway production, to start work on the film version in Astoria."

With the exception of Sylvia Sidney and Leif Erikson, the cast of the film version was composed entirely of stage actors rendering their lines and gestures in the style of their stage performance. The production (called a "scenario sermon well intentioned, if rather muddled" by John Coughlin of the *Motion Picture Herald*[21]) was overtly propagandistic. The thesis was an indictment of both slum landlords in New York and the system which allows the exploitation of the poor. The filmed version was hardly noticed. Although Frank Nugent in the *New York Times* gave it a good notice, he conceded that it lacked the "vitality" of the play.[22]

Toward the end of the next year, at the age of 16, the Maxwell Anderson play *Journey to Jerusalem* was also filmed, with Lumet playing his role as Joshua, the youthful Christ. The idea was conceived by Joseph Pollock, former president of the National Screen Service, who had planned to photograph the stage productions exactly as they were being performed on Broadway, using the original cast and scenic devices. Fox Movietone Studios financed the production as a deliberately photographed stage play, retaining all the details of the theatre without the intrusion of any cinematic invention; it was straightforward theatre-on-film. It was the first photographed stage play made available in 16mm exactly as produced by the Theatre Guild in New York. The appeal was almost exclusively oriented to church and civic groups.

"I loved being a child actor," Lumet relates. "I had ten rather marvelous years and it kept me off the streets."[23] Yet if Lumet loved acting in the theatre, he could also confess that "I *hated* acting in the movies, and I've understood all about actors ever since. That glass has a psychic and spiritual thing about it. The third eye. It's going to see something you don't want seen. I knew then that I could never be a really good [screen] actor."[24]

Divided as he was about acting on the stage and in the movies, the experience was formative for him. Two decades later he would become preoccupied with translating several theatrical masterpieces into "cinematic" versions, including *A View from the Bridge, Long Day's Journey into Night, The Sea Gull, Equus* and *The Wiz* — a preoccupation that would bring him both praise and criticism. Five of his first six films (which include a teleplay) and nearly half of his twenty-five features to date have their origins in the theatre.

During his years as a juvenile actor, Lumet attended Professional Children's School in New York, established for the irregular hours that child actors must keep. He entered Columbia University's extension department to concentrate on dramatic literature. His studies, however, ended abruptly after only one term, when at seventeen he enlisted in the Army Signal Corps as soon as America entered the Second World War. "I had always been extremely political," he explains. "I felt very passionately about the war, very committed." His service opportunities were restricted by his poor eyesight. Most of his duty during the war was concerned with the repair of radar devices and instruction for their use.

When he returned from duty in 1946, he succeeded Marlon Brando in the role of David in Ben Hecht's *A Flag is Born* at the Alvin Theatre. The play was staged to aid the American League for a Free Palestine. The story followed the post-war plight of the Jewish people to establish a homeland and pleaded for a Jewish consolidation. Kurt Weill composed the music and Luther Adler directed.

Of this period, Lumet remembers: "I knew at that time that if I stayed in acting, the best I could hope for was getting the part of the little Jewish kid from Brooklyn who got shot down by the mean Japs or Nazis, and then Clark Gable would pick me up and then with tears in his eyes would rush forward and single-handedly wipe out their machine gun nest. That was an area of drama that didn't particularly interest me."

Beginning in 1947, in rebellion against the work being done at the newly-formed Actors Studio, Lumet founded one of the first off-Broadway acting groups. He began with about a dozen actors (also renegades from the Actors Studio) and gradually attracted a score of others. His plan was a three-year project to study various acting styles. It was here that Lumet's ambitions went from acting to directing. "I discovered that there was nobody to direct. We'd formed a group of only actors, and so I began to direct — really because there was nobody else to do it." With his company Lumet staged off-beat plays, usually requiring no admission but relying on contributions. While his interest was with his acting group, Lumet (like the others) meagerly supported himself by teaching acting at the High School of Performing Arts and by working odd jobs in radio, television and theatre. "As training," he recalls, "it was probably as valuable as any I've ever had in my life."

While devoting his efforts and energies to directing, Lumet made one final return to acting. In 1948 he assumed the role of Tonya in Arthur Goodman's experimental play *Seeds in the Wind*, directed by Paul Tripp at the Empire Theatre. Like *A Flag Is Born*, this play also concerns the Jewish position. After the horrors of the Nazi massacre at Lidice, a colony of children (led by Tonya) band together to create an ideal world in which there are no hatreds, no wars and no national boundaries. This utopian commune functions smoothly until it is disrupted by the infectious presence of a corrupt adult. The highly political play drew the attention of the critics. Lumet received several favorable notices for his performance, such as the comment by Brooks Atkinson in the *New York Times* that "[Lumet] plays with exceptional force and clarity."[25]

At the age of twenty-six, after nearly two decades of acting and a few years of theatrical directing, Lumet was offered a position by CBS as an assistant director. "I'd been directing for close to two years, loved what I was doing, and a friend of mine [Yul Brynner] had become a staff director for CBS. 'The money is good,' Yul said. 'Come on in. Nobody knows what they're doing here anyway. We'll have a ball.' " Since television directing was comparatively new, a number of assistant directors were added to the networks. Lumet remembers that he and "Bobby" Mulligan were hired the same day by CBS. ("I remember us filling out our W-4 forms together.") "The work was absolutely invaluable. It's impossible to describe how many benefits we all derived from it," he recalls with affection.

A year later he graduated to the position of staff director. His first assignment was the *Danger* series, a thirty minute weekly program in which the craft of murder was dramatized. Between 1951 and 1953, Lumet directed about a hundred and fifty of the *Danger* episodes. Working at a tireless pace (often involved in different aspects of eight separate shows at the same time) brought Lumet an exceptional degree of creativity, as well as productivity. "The split concentration that it took," he maintains, "was not as brutal as it sounds. It was a great training ground. . . . It would take twenty films to learn what I learned from on-the-spot television."

While doing *Danger*, he also directed twenty-six shows for the *You Are There* series, recreating great moments in history, and a number of shows for the *Mama* series. Lumet's distinguished work on *Danger* led to assignments on other dramatic shows. He quickly became one of the most prolific and respected television talents, directing as many as five hundred shows over the ensuing decade. During his years in television, Lumet estimates that he worked with, "conservatively," at least two thousand actors. "I've probably worked with — and enjoyed working with — more actors than almost any other director. . . . I guess that's one of the reasons I'm considered such a good actor's director."

Beginning in 1953, Lumet entered into what Erik Barnouw has described in *Tube of Plenty* as the "anthology series" of live programming. Unlike the "formula-bound episodic series, the anthology series emphasized diversity. The play was the thing," according to Barnouw.[26] Lumet moved easily into this new domain, directing over two hundred teleplays for CBS-TV's *Playhouse 90*, NBC-TV's *Kraft Television Theatre* and *Studio One,* among others. Most of these were original teleplays that emanated live from New York. Lumet's background in theatre now served him well, since this form of television attracted theatrical guidelines. One of the shows with which Lumet was associated was Worthington Miner's *Studio One*. Most of the directors Miner recruited for the show had, like Lumet, experience in the theatre. Franklin Schaffner, George Roy Hill, Yul Brynner, Pat Nickell and Robert Mulligan all became prominent in *Studio One*. "In my directors," Miner relates, "I was looking for a theatrical set of standards. A respect for the literate word and the provocative idea."[27]

Recalling this period, Lumet refers to it as "the marvelous period in American television" [34]. Barnouw suggests that "one reason they were marvelous was that a producer, not a committee, was in control."[28] But as the years pass, Lumet remembers most the personal and professional challenges. We "faced only one limitation — our own competence. With fourteen hours of drama a week, a limited number of sets and minuscule budgets, we were able to experiment. If we laid an egg, it was a $20,000 egg, not the $300,000 one it would be today."[29]

During the mid and late fifties, television in America entered an era of enormous creative energy, often described as the "golden age" of live television. Such anthology dramas as *Play of the Week*, *Playhouse 90* and *Studio One* offered an exceptionally fertile training ground for young directors. Whenever Lumet speaks of his years in television, he does so with affection. "I am eternally grateful to television," he has said, "live television that is — which is a very different thing from what television has become — because of the opportunities it opened up.... I always feel basically lucky at having coincided with the historical accident of being ready to start directing when television was being born, because otherwise I think it would have been a very, very different and much more long and painful struggle."

Briefly interrupting his television career, Lumet made his debut as a stage director in January 1955 with the off-Broadway revival of Bernard Shaw's *The Doctor's Dilemma*, a satire on pomposity in the medical profession. It was received with mixed reviews by the critics. William Hawkins in the *New York World-Telegram* mentioned that "Lumet directs the play in an inventive, vivid style,"[30] while Walter Kerr of the *New York Herald Tribune* faulted Lumet as guiding the play and performers "into an upstage corner."[31] Despite the mixed reception, *The Doctor's Dilemma* proved to be one of the most successful productions at the Phoenix Theatre. And in December of the next year, Lumet directed Kermit Bloomgarden's production of Arch Oboler's imaginative science-fiction drama *Night of the Auk*, about five men in a space ship returning from the first successful journey to the moon to an earth beset by atomic war. Although the play starred such established actors as Claude Rains, Christopher Plummer, Wendell Corey and Dick York, it lasted only eight days at the Playhouse Theatre.

When television burst upon the cultural scene, Hollywood feared that their audience would be lured away by the glass box. Studios responded to the threat of television in several ways. One way was to exploit various technical innovations — like 3-D, Cinerama and CinemaScope — that television could not imitate. Another was to concentrate on wide-scale epics with massive budgets, locations, casts and lengths. Charlton Heston, for example, was parting the Red Sea in *The Ten Commandments* (1956) and would shortly mobilize young America against the French in *The Buccaneer* (1958), win the chariot race in *Ben-Hur* (1959) and unite Spain against the Moors in *El Cid* (1961). Television, obviously, couldn't compete with the lavish production values and public notoriety of, for example, *Cleopatra* (1959) and *The Longest Day* (1962); nor did television attempt to. A third way that studios reacted to combat the threat of television was, as a sort of security move, to devote an increasing portion of their own talent and facilities to servicing television series and to making films specifically for television. Warners, Fox, M-G-M and Columbia all became quite active in producing shows for televised viewing.

It was against this background that, in 1955, a modest little film, made in black-and-white with standard screen size, telling a simple story, and using unglamorous performers, suddenly and unexpectedly upset the entire film industry. The film was *Marty*. This solid and unpretentious film won Academy Awards for best picture, best actor (Ernest Borgnine), best director (Delbert Mann) and best screenplay (Paddy Chayefsky). What was perhaps most significant, and in its way quite revolutionary, was that the talent involved in making the film came directly from television. With *Marty*, which itself had originally been written and produced as a teleplay, Chayefsky and Mann proved that basic human drama was not only important, but could be commercially popular.

To articulate the intention of this revolution, it is useful to review Paddy Chayefsky's notes for *Marty*. "I tried to write the dialogue as if it had been wire-tapped," he explains, "I tried to envision the scenes as if a camera had been focused upon the unsuspecting characters and had caught them in an untouched moment of life."[32] (Chayefsky's words here sound very similar to some of the early manifestoes of Cesare Zavattini and the neo-realist movement a decade earlier.)

Imitating the teleplays of the "golden age," filmmakers discovered that the "small" subject and the "sensitive " treatment — utilizing the low budget, modest production and sharp perception — could make fine films that would draw audiences and would garner both critical and commercial attention. Such productions also meant that studios would not need to invest and risk their dwindling assets upon single epic ventures that could make or break a studio. The American cinema had tapped a vital new source of both meaning and talent — drawn, ironically, from television itself.

After the success of *Marty*, many notable television directors, like Mann, gravitated towards the expanded opportunities in feature films and made impressive debuts. In 1956, writer Robert Alan Aurthur and director Martin Ritt, both coming from television, combined to make *Edge of the City*. In the next year, Reginald Rose and Lumet made *Twelve Angry Men*, John Frankenheimer made *The Young Stranger*, Robert Mulligan made *Fear Strikes Out*, and Ritt made *No Down Payment*. And in 1958, Arthur Penn made *The Left-Handed Gun*. Rod Serling, who had been a writer for television, contributed a screenplay based on his teleplay *Patterns of Power* (1956). Chayefsky remained prolific with *The Bachelor Party* (1957) and *The Goddess* (1959), as did Reginald Rose with *Crime in the Streets* (1956) and *Man in the Net* (1959). (Franklin Schaffner, another talent from television who transferred to film, didn't make the transition until the early sixties with *The Stripper* and *The Best Man*.)

In live television, the director had to be highly versatile; he had to have expertise with actors, camera, design, lighting, timing, editing — he had to be as much a technician as a creator. He had to be comfortable with improvisation and split-second decision-making. And he learned by experiment, because, as Lumet says, "there were no rules about what could or could not be done." Lumet, always enthusiastic about this phase of his career, considers that what he learned about "the emotional meaning of lenses" and "the technical rules of editing" were the two most significant lessons from television.

For all the revitalizing that television-trained directors brought to filmmaking at this crucial time, there is a distinct *TV-style*, which for many years, according to many critics, characterized Hollywood. Set-ups, for example, are dictated by cramped sets, framing is often careless and tentative, close-ups are too frequently employed, and backgrounds are minimized. Yet as critic (later director) Tony Richardson rather optimistically noted in 1956: "The growth of television has in fact given Hollywood the possibility of something like neo-realist casting."[33] Or, as Pauline Kael pessimistically observed a decade later, "the immediacy of foreground action and as many climaxes as possible" [41]. Lumet, particularly, for years would be haunted and hounded by the critics (especially Kael) for his inability to develop beyond his television training.

Although Lumet had directed many of Reginald Rose's teleplays, especially on the popular *Danger* series, he had neither directed nor seen the televised production of *Twelve Angry Men* (Franklin Schaffner had directed the television version). Rose and Henry Fonda, who co-produced the film, commissioned Lumet to direct the film version.

The film offers us an intimate view of a jury as it must decide to convict or acquit a young boy accused of patricide. At the beginning it seems clear that the boy is guilty. Only one juror dissents at first, but eventually all the jurors come to acknowledge the presence of a "reasonable doubt." During the deliberations, the spiritual and mental complexions of the dozen men are gradually revealed.

Except for a brief prologue and equally brief epilogue, all the events take place in the jury room and adjoining washroom. Virtually all the film centers around the conference table, with minimal physical activity. Given the severe limitation of space and the rejection of flashbacks, the film could easily have slipped into tedium. Rather than playing it safe (with changes of scenery and pace, for example), Lumet carefully chose to emphasize the claustrophobic and oppressive environment of the single set.

With no dynamic physical action, he kept the camera on and around the jury table, using three hundred and eighty-five set-ups (which were shot totally out of sequence in the room). After twenty years, Lumet reflects on the film: "The point was to use the confinement, and not to expand the original TV script — or to open it up. What we did was to restrict it more and more from a visual point of view. As the film went on I used longer and longer lenses so that the ceiling became closer to the heads, the walls became closer to the chairs. I kept putting it into a smaller and smaller box to increase the claustrophobic feeling of it. . . . This was all achieved between the choice of lenses and the lighting" [53]. *Twelve Angry Men* was the first in a series of highly successful collaborations between Lumet and veteran photographer Boris Kaufman.

The film was completed in nineteen days, at a cost of $343,000. It received highly favorable critical acclaim, and Lumet was recognized as a director of definite promise. The film won Berlin's Golden Bear award, and Lumet won the Directors Guild award and was nominated for an Academy Award (he would have to wait eighteen years for his next nomination). Since he made *Twelve Angry Men*, Lumet has remained steadily in films — although never in Hollywood — with occasional diversions back into both theatre and television.

How did Lumet find working in films for the first time as a director? "The transition was primarily in aesthetic terms. Technically I was totally prepared by the time I hit my first movie. . . . There were no more technical mysteries, but there were enormous aesthetic ones. The biggest adjustment I had to make — and it took me many years to learn this — was the adjustment of scale — the size of the picture. Moving from a 17-inch piece of glass to a 35-foot screen meant that a story had to be told in an entirely different way. . . . The lenses remained the same, but the frame is so much more dynamic, accomplishes so much more for you so much more quickly."

Lumet's most successful single year as a television director was probably

1958. In this year, he directed three significant teleplays, all produced by David Susskind for the *Kraft Television Theatre,* and all of which drew important critical accolades. The first, an adaptation of three short plays by Tennessee Williams, was done in April. The second, an adaptation of Hemingway's *Fifty Grand,* was in May. And the third, an adaptation of Robert Penn Warren's *All the King's Men,* was in June. This last production was a rather daring venture, since Robert Rossen's film of the novel had won the Academy Award for Best Picture a decade earlier.

Lumet had distinguished himself with *Twelve Angry Men* as a filmmaker of the future. But his next three films, each of which was successively more ambitious, failed to sustain the promise of his first feature.

Stage Struck is a contemporary refurbishing of the Katherine Hepburn vehicle *Morning Glory.* Hepburn had won the Academy Award for her touching performance in the 1933 film. Lumet had not seen the original before making *Stage Struck* — "I didn't dare," he commented some years later [53]. As he had done in *Twelve Angry Men*, Henry Fonda both produced and starred. But unlike *Twelve Angry Men, Stage Struck* was a dismal critical and commercial failure. Lumet believes the film was ruined by the miscasting of Susan Strasberg (daughter of Lee Strasberg of the Actors Studio) and the weakness of her performance.

If it is weak as a film, especially when compared to *Morning Glory,* the film does exhibit Lumet's affection for the theatrical world of New York. *Stage Struck* is a highly personal tribute to Broadway. Lumet admits the failure of the film, especially at the box-office. "One of the reasons I wanted to do it so badly was that I love the theatre. I came from the theatre. And this was a sort of Valentine to the theatre, with its fairy tale of the understudy going on, which I'm very moved by. I wanted to make it a lovely little souffle of a movie, but I'm afraid I came up with a bit of a pancake" [53].

Like *Stage Struck,* Lumet's next film was a romantic tale set in New York. But unlike *Stage Struck, That Kind of Woman* was the simple story of a woman caught between two men, one offering her comfort and the other love. The plot line, rather predictably, hinges on whether she'll choose the rich older man or the poor but handsome soldier. "I did *That Kind of Woman,*" Lumet relates, "because I was enchanted with Sophia Loren."[34]

Carlo Ponti produced the film to provide an American vehicle for his wife, Loren, and to capitalize on the popularity of Tab Hunter. Although it was shot in New York, it was sent to Hollywood for scoring and re-cutting. According to Lumet, it was there that the film lost the simplicity and charm he wanted for it. Other damage was done by the rigid supervision of Ponti. "Ponti and I didn't get along," Lumet told an interviewer in 1965. "I'm sick about that film," he explained again in 1975. "The best scenes were cut out and the weak ones were left in and overemphasized by the editing and score . . . so shoot me."[35]

Why did Lumet make both *Stage Struck* and *That Kind of Woman*, two pieces so obviously inferior to *Twelve Angry Men*? "I could do them both in New York. It seems like a stupid excuse for doing a movie, but at the time it wasn't. I have no regrets about it. I'm sorry the pictures weren't better . . . they both could have been a lot better than they were" [34]. In part, doing all three of his first films in that city (as with Elia Kazan) was a deliberate effort to prove that filmmaking could be successfully accomplished in New York, and to promote more such activity in the city.

After *That Kind of Woman*, Lumet refused an offer to direct the film version of *A Raisin in the Sun* because it would have meant working in Hollywood. "I can wait," he told a reporter for the *New York Times* in 1960. "I feel I can improve by staying in the East, and there's always television and Broadway to pay my expenses. I'll let Hollywood come to me."[36] His early dislike for Hollywood was based upon the lack of independence, the inflated production costs and the less congenial working facilities.

In an interview for *Sight and Sound,* shortly after the release of *That Kind of Woman,* Lumet told Gene Moskowitz that he can work *only* at "white heat" and that his "form of inspiration is the energy generated by continuous, dynamic work." For the first time, Lumet had begun, rather cautiously, to formulate and articulate publicly his thoughts about filmmaking — largely drawn from his television experiences. He told Moskowitz that "a rediscovery of the dramatic and emotional possibilities of the close-up is one of the good things that television has begun to bring back to the cinema" and that "television thinking can bring a new firmness of progression and theme, provided it does not stifle the film's natural breadth and range" [27].*

Even if *Stage Struck* and *That Kind of Woman* were unsuccessful, Lumet's first three films did bring him to the attention of cineastes and film journals. In April 1959, for example, Lumet contributed an article to *Cahiers du Cinéma* in which he discussed his philosophy of directing. "The maturity of a director," he wrote, "resides in his capacity to choose what is best for the whole rather than his desire to make the work a perfect expression of his own ego." Defending the importance of camera work as one of the most essential assets that a director has, he also suggested, "I don't think the beautiful image should draw attention to itself. The beauty of the camera work resides in its discrete plastic contribution to the dramatic whole" [77].*

Lumet's next film, *The Fugitive Kind,* created considerable controversy. It

---

*It is interesting to anticipate that many of the characteristics of television Lumet applauds in this interview are the identical characteristics that Pauline Kael would accuse him of not outgrowing in her article on *The Group* seven years later.

*My translation from the French.

was his first attempt to film a play from an acknowledged playwright — the first of two plays Lumet would film from the pen of Tennessee Williams.

Williams had originally written *Battle of Angels* in 1940. It failed then, as did his re-write in 1957 under the title *Orpheus Descending*. It is the downbeat tale of a disillusioned nightclub entertainer from New Orleans who drifts into a small Mississippi town where he becomes romantically involved with the wife of the owner of the local general store. The film begins in a violent rainstorm and ends in a destructive fire; it begins in hope and ends in despair. On the thematic level, Lumet consciously opted to strive for realism rather than mythology.

According to Maurice Yacowar, who has analyzed all the filmed version of Williams' plays, the film alters the play in two significant ways: "the element of allegorical abstraction in the play is subordinated to the physical realism of the film," and "Lumet increases Val's visibility and his influence upon the other characters." By implementing these two major structural changes, Lumet thus heightened the personal involvement, and the "film achieves a greater emotional impact by playing the original horrors against a more realistic surface."[37] This alteration obviously required substantial re-writing and re-staging (not always in harmony with Williams). "From the very beginning," states cinematographer Boris Kaufman, "it was essential to inject a dour and foreboding atmosphere of impending doom, reminiscent of the remote but implicit legend of Orpheus descending into Hell."[38]

From the outset, however, the project was plagued with difficulties. Brando "was fat but gorgeous." Anna Banana (as Lumet affectionately calls her) had severe problems with her English articulation and had to do her part mostly from phonetics. She also "couldn't be photographed on her left side at all" according to Lumet.[39] There were many bouts of temperament with the performers, disagreements with Williams over the re-writes (Williams later attacked Lumet for his mis-direction), a disastrous sneak preview at which Williams was actually booed by the audience (December 1959), and a massive re-cutting, which deleted some twenty-five minutes from the film. Lumet admits, looking back on the film, that "If we had set out to create a disaster, we couldn't have done a better job." Yet the critics were not so unanimously unkind. Derek Hill in the *London Tribune* perhaps typified the critical consensus: "Sidney Lumet and the brilliant team of Marlon Brando and Anna Magnani have so courageously ignored the absence of straw that the bricks they construct often give an effective illusion of solidarity."[40]

After filming *The Fugitive Kind*, Lumet said, in an interview with Peter Bogdanovich, "I hope *The Fugitive Kind* makes a lot of money, because none of my pictures have made a lot of money and I *need* one. I know my employment will be directly affected by it" [30]. This was not uttered in desperation or spite, but more in appraisal of the realities of the market — a consistent complaint that Lumet subsequently reiterated on many other occasions (i.e., that the method of financing and distributing feature films either precludes or restricts individual creativity).

Although *The Fugitive Kind* didn't make a lot of money, neither did it terminate his employment. While doing *Stage Struck* and *The Fugitive Kind*, Lumet and Reginald Rose fought to do a film called *Black Monday*, the story of a Southern town on the first day of school integration. The project was rejected because the studios feared that it would not make money.

Even while directing films, Lumet continued occasional stage productions. In February 1960, he staged the spectacular Broadway version of Albert Camus' brooding philosophical drama about the murderous and monstrous Roman Emperor, *Caligula*, who used his unlimited powers in an attempt to achieve the impossible. Camus had long refused to grant permission for his play to be staged in America, convinced that it would be inadequately produced and presented. He conceded to have it done under Lumet's realization. When it appeared and was reviewed, the production was variously regarded from "magnificent" to "provocative" to "stimulating failure." Frank Aston of the *New York World-Telegram* represented most critics when he wrote, "All praise is due Sidney Lumet for his heated, lucid direction."[41]

After the failure of *The Fugitive Kind*, Lumet returned to some television work. In a final effort to keep television drama alive, the use of "documentary drama" (plays based on true incidents) became popular with the *Armstrong Circle Theatre* for NBC. In June 1960, Lumet's taped program of *The Sacco and Vanzetti Story* was aired. It starred Martin Balsam as Sacco and Steven Hill as Vanzetti, and co-starred Peter Falk and E. G. Marshall. Written by Reginald Rose, the two-part semi-documentary was immediately controversial. Not only was it well received, but it earned Lumet a nomination for the Emmy award from the National Academy of Television Arts and Sciences (NATAS).

Then, in November of the same year, Lumet directed his classic treatment of Eugene O'Neill's *The Iceman Cometh*, featuring Jason Robards, Jr. in the leading role of Theodore Hickman. The four hour production was first presented on WNTA-TV on the celebrated *Play of the Week* series. This version of *The Iceman Cometh* was controversial because of the gritty language that spiced the dialogue. It was produced by Ely Landau, then Chairman of the National Telefilm Associates (owners of WNTA-TV and producers of *Play of the Week)*, and won Lumet the NATAS Emmy.

Lumet considers *The Iceman Cometh* his most challenging TV production. He told interviewer John Shanley of the *New York Times*, "I'm terribly curious to see whether we can get genuine tragedy on television — on a 21-inch piece of glass. Size is a consideration. Half the problem of reality in motion pictures is solved because your senses are overwhelmed by size. And in the theatre you need the artifice of a proscenium arch."[42] O'Neill's widow, Carlotta Monterey O'Neill, was so impressed by the production that she awarded Lumet the rights to all subsequent productions of O'Neill's plays over which she had control.

From December of that year through February of the next year, Lumet directed four productions for NBC's *Play of the Week* for Landau: *Rashomon, The Dybbuk, John Brown's Raid* and *Cry Vengeance*. When he returned to making films, Lumet chose as his next project Arthur Miller's *A View from the Bridge*. It was a play about a Brooklyn longshoreman's distorted and doomed attraction for his wife's niece. Raf Vallone had played the role of Eddie Carbone on the Paris stage and was suggested for the movie role by Miller. As in *The Fugitive Kind*, Lumet selected a realistic (rather than mythological) approach to the play, to minimize its obvious implications of Greek tragedy.

The exteriors were filmed on the docks of Brooklyn and the interiors in a Paris studio. "That was sheerly financial," Lumet explains. "The man who bought it had a few dollars and many francs. So we spent the dollars doing the exteriors in America and the francs on the interiors in Paris. But it worked out marvelously" [34].

When the film was released, it, like his previous films, got a generally favorable reception but failed to make its return at the box-office. Isabel Quigly in the *Spectator* wrote, "Sidney Lumet, who was one of the white hopes of the American outburst of realism in the cinema a few years ago, . . . has done an interesting job filming Arthur Miller's *A View from the Bridge*. It could, of course, have turned into a very different sort of film, but Lumet, above all an honest and unfrilly director, has the temperament to dampen rather than fan hysteria and frightfulness, to give a feeling of enclosure and concentration to make tragedy domestic."[43]

In 1962 Lumet began work on the film he has repeatedly claimed to be his personal favorite. Writing in *Movie People*, in 1968, Lumet said: "I can tell you quite honestly that *Long Day's Journey into Night* is the best movie I've ever made" [82]. It was produced, again by Ely Landau, and made for less than $500,000, primarily because the actors were willing to participate for nominal salaries and shares of the proceeds. No scriptwriter was engaged, since the decision was made to keep the film version totally faithful to O'Neill's play. Like *Twelve Angry Men*, the spatial parameters were restricted almost exclusively to the confines of a single set — the Tyrone living room.

In transferring the play to film, Lumet utilized the close-up and camera angles to dramatize the tensions which alienate the family members. Again working with Boris Kaufman to devise a highly expressive sense of photographic comment, Lumet describes an experiment he made after *Long*

Day's Journey into Night had been finished. Taking a frame enlargement of the first close-up for each of the four principals and comparing them to a corresponding frame enlargement of the last close-up for each, Lumet claims "that looking at them next to one another on a screen from a still projector, the faces were almost unrecognizable; you would have had difficulty recognizing them as the same person."

The film was entered in the Cannes Film Festival, where all four principal players won top acting honors. Lumet received the Directors Guild Award. The film was either emphatically hailed as a masterpiece or condemned as merely filmed theatre. Most of the praise, however, was given to the acting rather than Lumet's direction.

Of all his films, it is perhaps this one that Lumet has defended most ardently against his detractors who contend that it is merely a photographed stage play. In a 1962 article for the *New York Times*, for example, Lumet stated, "In the original text there were four characters in the play. What makes *Long Day's Journey* a film rather than a photographed stage play is a fifth character added to the movie: the camera. . . . Interestingly enough, from a purely technical point of view, the cinematic attack on *Long Day's Journey* is far more difficult, complex, and subtle than is needed on a normal film. . . . [The] technical virtuosity that must be found to reveal the drama, demand far greater film technique than usual" [78]. Even in a 1965 interview Lumet was still defending the film. "All their [the critics'] eyes were capable of seeing was scenery; they didn't know cinema technique from a hole in the wall. There was more sheer physical technique in that movie, in its editing and its camerawork, than anything you are liable to see for 20 years" [34].

Late in 1962, Lumet returned to the theatre and directed the James Lipton-Sol Berkowitz musical *Nowhere To Go But Up*. Dorothy London, Martin Balsam and Tom Bosley played the leads with Mary Ann Mobley, the former Miss America, in the nostalgic look at the Prohibition era. Receiving generally unfavorable notices from the critics, the play had a short engagement at the Winter Garden.

Fail Safe, an adaptation of Eugene Burdick and Harvey Wheeler's bestselling novel about the hazards of accidental nuclear warfare, was financed privately. It began as a project of Max Youngstein, a former United Artists executive who wanted to launch a New York production company on the basis of profit participation. He interested Lumet and John Frankenheimer in the concept, and *Fail Safe* was to be the first in a five film package to establish the company.

In an interview for *Newsday*, Lumet said, "We're suddenly living with things that are out of control. All of a sudden we're helpless. We can't do anything. They're [sic] ain't no answers. The machines are big; they're bigger than we are. . . . Well, I'm not going to leave it to an IBM machine whether I'm going to be blown sky-high or not. Not if I can help it."[44]

Although *Fail Safe* was entered in the New York Film Festival, it was severely hurt commercially by the release of Stanley Kubrick's *Dr. Strangelove*. Both films were being shot simultaneously, *Fail Safe* in New York and *Dr. Strangelove* in England. Lumet revealed afterwards that "I didn't know anything about it [*Dr. Strangelove*] until we'd finished shooting and were sued. . . . I knew we were dead as a movie as soon as Columbia bought us, because I knew they had done that to hold us off until *Dr. Strangelove* was released" [53].

The first commercial blockbuster for Lumet came in 1965 with the release of *The Pawnbroker*. Based on Edwin Lewis Wallant's novel, the film was almost universally praised by the critics for its skill and daring. Lumet claims that "The thing I am happy about in this film is that it is a real breaking of the conventional hero idea; the man is an absolute bastard, the people around him are in general totally unpleasant, there is no sentimentalizing about Jews or Negroes . . ." [80]. *The Pawnbroker* appeared on nearly every top film list for the year, Rod Steiger won the best acting award in the Berlin Film Festival competition, and Lumet won the British Academy Award for his direction.

Lumet had come to the project rather late — two weeks before shooting was scheduled to begin. The former director had to be relieved because of illness, and Landau, who produced the film, asked Lumet to direct it. With the exception of Steiger, who was already committed to the film, the casting and locations were all completed in two weeks. For many of the performers, (including Jaime Sanchez, who plays Ortiz) it was their first film.

One of the most controversial techniques used in the film was the quick shock cuts — at first using one, two, three frame cuts that gradually progress and build to six and then eventually to a complete segment — to reveal Nazerman's awakening consciousness. In the book, Nazerman's past is reconstructed through his dreams. It was Lumet's decision to use the shock cuts rather than dream fragments. "As far as I know," Lumet asserted in 1973, "it was the first time it was used and it came out of the precise way my own memory works. I literally, if I'm trying to block something out, find it cropping up in little tiny bursts, little tiny flashes" [49].

In addition to the shock cuts, Lumet experimented with improvisation. This was necessary, he maintains, because of the many painful script difficulties. "My favorite scene in the picture is completely improvised; the scene between the boy and his mother when she's cooking for him and he's in the bathtub. That wasn't even in the script" [82].

Called "unnatural naturalism" by Lumet, the film had difficulty collecting its Production Code Seal. The objection raised about the film centered around the scene in which the black prostitute bares her breasts to entice Nazerman. Joseph L. Mankiewicz organized a group of several directors to formally protest the original denial of the Seal. The Seal was granted and the scene retained.

The Pawnbroker was exactly what Lumet's career needed at the moment. "It was one of the surprises of my life that *The Pawnbroker* turned out to be such an enormous commercial success. Because, of course, I just don't know what makes a commercial success, but it was my first really big grosser" [53]. The film brought Lumet a deluge of notoriety and distinction, which continued with *The Hill*.

The Hill was based upon screenwriter Ray Rigby's play about his own experiences when imprisoned in a similar military detention camp during the Second World War. The brutal and uncompromising film centers around the busted RSM sent to the prison camp on a degrading and exhausting punishment course and his clash with the dehumanizing regimentation and sadism of the system. To enhance the sense of physical exertion involved, "the hill" was literally constructed on the set. It took two months to build, was thirty-five feet high, composed of sand and rock, and inclined on a sixty degree angle.

As in many of his films, Lumet injected his own sense of realism. "*The Hill*," he recalls, "was an attempt at a naturalistic picture, and I felt that it should be made naturalistic at all levels" [82]. In the original ending of the play, for example, the prisoners won their final victory over the system. "Now that, of course, is nonsense," comments Lumet. "We know that in most areas the establishment really keeps control, and nobody is going to tell me that in an army, much less a prison, that isn't going to happen. . . . The ending was deliberately caustic" [82].

Although the film takes place in a military stockade in Northern Africa, it was shot on a vast stretch of desert near Almeria in southern Spain and at M-G-M's Elstree studios in England. It was completed in forty-four days (three days ahead of schedule) at a cost of about $1,350,000 (some $50,000 under budget). It was Lumet's first experience in European filming, using (except for Ossie Davis) a British cast. It initiated a fondness for Europe, Sean Connery and Harry Andrews, both of whom would reappear in many of Lumet's future films.

The Hill was Britain's entry into the Cannes Festival. The film did well in Europe but fared less successfully in the United States. Although critical opinion was divided, audiences complained about the unintelligibility of the British voices. *The Hill* didn't diminish any of Lumet's growing prestige, but neither did the film expand it.

Certainly one of the most challenging projects for Lumet was the filming of Mary McCarthy's best-selling sensational novel of eight Vassar girls in the early years of the Depression. *The Group* follows the girls from the idealistic aspirations of their graduation day through the various compromises and failures over the next half decade. It was Lumet's most ambitious film thus far, with a longer shooting schedule and bigger budget than he had previously had. The budget was set at better than $2½ million, which was not only Lumet's most expensive film but also the most expensive film yet to be made in New York.

"I fear the worst," speculated Mary McCarthy (a self-confessed non-filmgoer) from Paris a month before *The Group* was to open in New York.[45] Lumet countered by calling her novel "a structural disaster. If I'd read it first [i.e., before the screenplay], I would not have made the movie. . . . In the movie, we haven't changed the plot, but we've put the humanity back."[46]

Despite the many academic debates that ensued over the differences between the novel and the film, *The Group* did well at the box-office. But, like so many of his previous films, it was received with mixed (although generally unfavorable) reviews. Rather than Lumet's direction, however, it was Sidney Buchman's script that bore the brunt of critical reaction. Penelope Gilliatt, writing in London's *Sunday Observer*, represented many critics when she observed, "Buchman's script is disconcertingly scrappy, as though one were watching installments in a woman's serial; tiny cliff-hanging climaxes are reached every so often, the tone skids into chattiness, and then a whole new episode begins."[47]

During the making of *The Group* in the Spring of 1966, film critic Pauline Kael was invited to observe the entire production — from scripting to casting to rehearsing to shooting to editing to preview. In her lengthy essay on "The Making of *The Group*" for the *New Yorker*, she bears down hard on both the film and th director. Although finding Lumet personally likable, she faults him for his apparent lack of sensitivity to the novel's original sardonic tone (which she liked) and for his habitual adherence to the television orientation approach to filmmaking (which she didn't like). "He'll go on faking it," she writes of him, "using the abilities he has to cover up what he doesn't know; he'll go on using space as stage space hyped up with a few tricks, treating movies as just a bigger canvas than TV. For even his honesty about his limitations is probably the result of his not really thinking they are limitations." Yet with that touch of sarcasm and perception that has characterized her writing, Kael concludes that "by the time *The Group* was finished everybody knew he was going to be a big director" [41].

In a 1967 article for *Film Quarterly*, Graham Petrie discusses Lumet's career in one of the first extended critical pieces on the director. Petrie seems to voice the collective view of Lumet at the time. "Most critics seem to sense that something about Lumet's films commands respect, or ought to; yet there seem to be too many obstacles in the way of wholehearted recognition of him as a first-rate director" [40]. Petrie continues to assess Lumet's work with both theatrical and literary adaptations and the special problems involved in realizing them on the screen. Petrie's pioneering article began to confront issues over a wide range of films that critics of Lumet's individual films seemed unable to define or measure.

After *The Group*, Lumet hurried off to London again in February 1966, to begin filming John Le Carre's first novel, under the title of *The Deadly Affair*. This mood spy drama marked Lumet's debut as a producer. Like virtually all of his other films, this one was shot with meticulous planning and compression in eight weeks (a week under schedule). The budget for the film was set at slightly under $1¼ million.

In *The Deadly Affair*, Lumet selected, as he had done so often before, a realistic approach to capture and convey the realistic theme in this somber de-glamorized perspective of spying. In an interview in *Variety*, Lumet laments that the film could not have been made in black-and-white. The pressures from television now demanded that any film financed by a major American studio be made in color. Lumet calls this "the enormous loss of another filmmaking tool." He maintains that the gritty and subtle texture of black-and-white was more realistic than the "maytime" effect of color. But, he continues, this regrettable situation could have a stimulating benefit *if* cinematographers were encouraged to experiment with new dimensions in color photography.[48]

The Deadly Affair was not the first film to explore various color properties. John Huston's *Moby Dick* (1956), for example, used a "double printing" process, printing Technicolor stock with an overlay of black-and-white stock to mute the color strains throughout the film. Unfortunately, according to Lumet, this method only succeeded in eliminating the red portion of the color spectrum, which could have been accomplished with a filter. But Lumet wanted a process that would reduce the saturation of each color on the stock without distorting or eliminating any.

"I wanted a simple, realistic movie in a very natural sort of color," Lumet stated [82]. To do this, he and cinematographer Freddie Young, famed for his two previous Academy Awards, devised a process — technically called "pre-flashing" — to mute the colors by pre-exposing a color negative film stock before rather than after shooting,* thereby permitting a more subtle effect. Lumet dubbed the process "colorless color" and explained, "I can tell you that this way we can knock out the glamour. The phony edge is taken off and everything is real."[49] The result was to minimize the top and bottom of the color register without loss of definition. In an article in *American*

---

*One important reason for doing it *before* shooting rather than afterwards in the lab was that it assures the desired effect and prevents the likely possibility of a later studio decision to retain the bright colors of the Technicolor process—which would be the studio's prerogative and right.

Cinematographer, Young comments that "this method does not change the colour values in any way, it merely softens or subdues colour . . . and personally I feel the colour is more true to life generally speaking."[50]

At this juncture in his career, having made eleven features in nine years, Lumet was being recognized and discussed for his ability to extract consistent, powerful performances. In reviewing *The Deadly Affair,* for example, Richard Roud suggested that "The one talent that has never deserted the director throughout his strange career — as many downs as ups — is his handling of actors."[51]

With *Twelve Angry Men, Long Day's Journey into Night, Fail Safe, The Pawnbroker* and *The Deadly Affair,* Lumet seemed to be reaching for serious subjects. With *Bye, Bye Braverman* and *The Sea Gull,* both smaller in scale, Lumet entered a brief period of highly personal films.

Bye, Bye Braverman is, according to Lumet, "the most personal picture I've ever made. . . . These four post-Depression Jewish intellectuals are everyone I grew up with. Me, in fact."[52] Based on humorist Wallace Markfield's highly praised first novel *To an Early Grave,* the film is a dark and irreverent comedy about four friends who embark on a misguided journey through Brooklyn to the funeral of a close friend. On the way to Leslie Braverman's funeral, the four encounter, among other obstacles, a black Jewish cab driver and attend a session at the wrong funeral parlor.

Lumet, as a child, had lived across the street from the "East Park Memorial" synagogue (actually the Madie Payton House) on Easter Parkway near Rochester Avenue. "Scouting locations for this film," Lumet muses, "was a cinch. I know all these neighborhoods like the back of my hand. It must have taken me about five minutes to scout the whole works."[53] Not only Lumet but everyone involved in the production seemed personally dedicated to it. George Segal worked for a fraction of his usual salary, as did most of the others.

Strongly based upon American Jewish humor, *Bye, Bye Braverman* was a risky commercial venture from the outset. Lumet has repeatedly commented, "I thought the script was perfect and charming, although the critics kicked the Hell out of the completed film" [82]. Some critics thought the film overdone and self-indulgent, others thought it tasteless or pointless; practically no one applauded it. Commenting on the film some ten years later, Lumet criticized himself: "Let me put it this way: I think it was one of the best scripts I've ever received, but felt that my own work didn't match it. My control wasn't firm enough, I wasn't in command, and I edited it badly. . . . At the same time I loved it, and . . . know in my heart of hearts that there was more to be gotten out of that material" [53].

The Sea Gull was another highly personal project for Lumet. It was his third English production and reunited four of the stars from *The Deadly Affair,* James Mason, Simone Signoret, David Warner and Harry Andrews.

Lumet has frequently referred to it as one of his finest and favorite films. "The only two films I've made in which I wouldn't change a thing," he once reflected, "are *Long Day's Journey* and *The Sea Gull*."[54] Although it was a faithful rendering of Chekhov's play and an obvious labor of love, it fared poorly at the box-office and with the reviewers. Leading the critical attack was Hollis Alpert in the *Saturday Review:* "I looked forward to seeing *The Sea Gull*, with its impressive cast, and found myself badly disappointed. How is it possible for a play that reads so well, and is sometimes performed well on stage, to come out as an excruciating bore on film?"[55]

A major fault that many critics found with Lumet's adaptation was his mishandling of Chekhov's humor. The anonymous reviewer for *Time* commented that "Chekhov called *The Sea Gull* a comedy, but any traces of wit have been pretty well destroyed by Lumet's lumbering technique."[56] Peter Cowie, while awarding Lumet the honor of being named one of the five top international directors for 1968 in the *International Film Guide*, later observed that "The wit of Chekhov's play eludes Lumet, for all his worthy, competent rendering of the major scenes and his respectful camera style."[57] One of the kinder reactions came from Margaret Hinxman in the *Sunday Telegraph;* despite her dissatisfaction with the result, she was able to write, "It must be said, though, that Sidney Lumet is incapable of making an unattractive film."[58]

Following the critical and commercial disappointment of *The Sea Gull*, Lumet made what is probably his least successful film. *The Appointment* was made in Rome with two internationally favorite stars. Omar Sharif had been a matinee idol since his appearance in *Lawrence of Arabia* (1962), and Anouk Aimée was still fondly remembered for her role in *A Man and A Woman* (1966). Yet despite the romantic leads and lavish production values, the weakness of the story defeated the film.

Lumet called *The Appointment* "the story of a man who chases an aberration. . . . a masochistic love story";[59] the critics called it "a flimsy love story which never really catches fire" and "uninventively directed." Hawk in *Variety* regretted that "Flat writing and an over-rigid performance by Sharif in a crucial role, which at times skirts the laughable, seriously flaws what might otherwise have been an intriguing love tale cum suspenser."[60] The film was screened at the 1970 Cannes Film Festival and was received, according to Rex Reed, "with great hostility and even some derisive laughter."[61] After the disastrous entry and reception, *The Appointment* was heavily re-edited and all but shelved by M-G-M.

After the dismal and forgettable version of *The Appointment*, Lumet made another commercial failure. *Last of the Mobile Hot-Shots* was rather loosely based on Tennessee Williams' play *The Seven Descents of Myrtle* (published as *Kingdom of Earth*), which had opened in New York in March of 1968 but lasted only a month. In the course of transferring the play to film, Lumet made several significant changes. One was to "shift its emphasis from the theme of survival to an anatomy of racism," according to Maurice Yacowar in his study of the filmed version of Williams' plays.[62] The religious theme of the play was removed, and the social-racist theme of the film expanded. Another alteration resulted in a comic irony. In the play there are references to "rumors" of Chicken's black blood. Instead of using a Caucasian for the role of Chicken, as was usual, Lumet cast black actor Robert Hooks for the role.

In much the same vein as with his three previous films, the critics almost universally condemned *Last of the Mobile Hot-Shots*. The reviewer for *Time*, for example, reported that "The real tragedy of the *Last of the Mobile Hot-Shots* is that its failure comes not from the text, flawed as it is, but from the ignoble adaptation."[63] Like the critics, Williams found the film "perfectly disastrous."[64] Lumet also admitted its failings. "It was an extraordinary story. . . . It wasn't a success. But my feelings are that I would rather do incomplete Tennessee Williams than complete-anybody-else. It was lovely to work on and I'm sorry I couldn't solve it" [53]. Yacowar is less unkind than others. He suggests that "we must give Lumet his due. He wholeheartedly reshaped the material to support the redirection he chose to give the play. . . . All in all," Yacowar concludes, "the film is a provocative minor work by a major American director."[65]

As if starting the decade of the seventies afresh, after a series of poorly received films, Lumet discussed his films and critics in an article in *Variety*. In the article, he proclaims, "I don't fancy myself as The Second Coming. A director should always check himself, go back and look at his work as objectively as possible to see how it holds up and where he might have gone wrong." He continues in the article to rebuke the New York critics for deriding his films "from *Long Day's Journey* to *The Sea Gull* to *Bye, Bye Braverman*." Lumet's sharpest counterattack on the critics is based upon the premise that the critics lack the necessary knowledge of film technique to adequately or fairly evaluate the merits of a film. "You might say," he suggests rather defensively, "the major New York critics are deliberately laying for individual directors."[66]

Perhaps because of the critical and commercial failures of his last several projects, Twentieth-Century Fox delayed the appropriations for what was to be Lumet's next film, *Nat Turner*. The film was budgeted for $4 million, and allegedly Fox had already invested some $1.5 million. While waiting for a decision from Fox, Lumet assisted Ely Landau with his massive compilation documentary on the struggle of Martin Luther King. Along with Joseph L. Mankiewicz, Lumet directed the "connecting sequences" for *King: A Filmed Record*, in which top film personalities read inspirational passages at vital points in the compiled footage.

"It's a changed world," warns a fellow inmate to the departing safecracker at the beginning of *The Anderson Tapes*, Lumet's next project. After ten years in prison, it is indeed a changed world for Duke Anderson, and, ironically, it is that change which inadvertently foils the team of heisters in their master plan to loot a fashionable New York apartment house. In the film, two simultaneous and parallel levels are explored. On the plot level, the film is a daring and detailed caper — from planning to execution — that goes sour. Although it is hardly a unique plot, the iconographic level probes the increasing encroachment by concealed electronic surveillance devices which secretly invade and monitor the individual privacy of all, criminals and innocents alike.

The ending of *The Anderson Tapes*, according to a report in *Variety*,[67] was altered in the release version. The original ending has the gang of thieves successfully loot the posh dwelling. The police are alerted by the invalid boy who signals them by shortwave transmission, but the gang escapes. They are pursued in their huge van by police heliocopters and are trapped inside the Queens tunnel. As the police close in on them, they evade capture by using a station wagon concealed inside the van. The change, whereby the crooks are trapped inside the building and are all subsequently killed or captured, was apparently dictated because Columbia didn't want to jeopardize the future sale of the film to television where, it seems, a more rigid moral justice (i.e., crime doesn't pay) is required.

The film was enjoyed and acceped, though not praised, by most critics. After the series of failures that preceded *The Anderson Tapes*, John Russell Taylor felt renewed. Writing in the London *Times*, Taylor announced that "*The Anderson Tapes* comes as a happy reminder of how good he [Lumet] can be if he sets his mind to it and if his subject-matter is not too pretentious: in fact it is probably his best film since *The Deadly Affair*."[68] Taylor's enthusiasm, however, was not universal. Andrew Sarris of the *Village Voice* thought "there were about 11 good minutes in it, and the rest [was] confused and uncertain." (But Sarris also confesses that "the caper genre has never exactly entranced me.") "As for Sidney Lumet's laboriously impersonal direction of the project," Sarris continues, "let us say that this latest style without style has not yet attained the polished professionalism of William Wyler nor the clumsy sincerity of Stanley Kramer."[69]

In 1970 Lumet contributed a piece about the function of the film director to an anthology on the movie industry. His article in *Movie People* summarizes much of his feeling to that point. "Well, if you're a director, then you've got to direct. I don't believe that you should sit back and wait until circumstances are perfect before you and it's all gorgeous and marvelous. I did one really marvelous picture, one really first-rate picture, and two talented ones. All the choices were mine. I never did a picture because I was hungry; I could always earn mine in television. Every picture I did was an active, believable, passionate wish. Every picture I did I wanted to do. What may be a sort of self-deception is that everything I did was also always an effort to get to something else. . . . I'm having a good time. I lead a nice life. Great!" [82].

Lumet's next project was, again, an adaptation of a successful stage play. *Child's Play* tells the sinister story of unexplained and seemingly senseless violence in a Catholic boarding school for boys. The violence, however, as we discover, is only the residual projection of a desperate struggle between two strong-willed teachers in the school.

Certainly the improbable situation and ambiguous resolution damaged the credibility and reception of the film for both audiences and critics. Equally damaging may have been the release in the same year of William Friedkin's *The Exorcist*, which immediately and completely overshadowed any other film that alluded to satanism. Whatever the reason, *Child's Play* received only limited distribution and attention. Michael McKegney in the *Village Voice*, however, complained that ". . . Sidney Lumet's mise en scene comes unstuck under the strain of its stylistic contradictions long before the final diabolical fadeout."[70]

The Offence was the third collaboration between Lumet and Sean Connery, who had just been voted Britain's top box-office star. The film was made in England for Tantalion Productions, a production company partly owned by Connery, who plays the lead in this grim, violent and unpleasant character study based on John Hopkins' play *This Story of Yours*. It is an intensive and searching study of a psychotic police officer who, under the strain of internalizing the effects of his job and enduring an unsatisfying marriage, has become more dangerous than the suspect he interrogates. His psychosis is brought on by his twenty years of dedicated service investigating violent and grotesque crimes and the accumulated effect these horrors have on his mind.

The film is slow, careful and ambiguous. It is, as Richard Schickel notes in his review for *Time* magazine, "less a whodunit than a whydunit." Schickel objects to the stylistic gloss, and he comments that "Lumet's direction strives to give to material that is neither edifying nor suspenseful a fake profundity, stretching it to unconscionable lengths."[71] But Margaret Hinxman of the *Sunday Telegraph* compliments the film, because "The acting is as finely judged as it always is in a Lumet film."[72]

"I decided I wanted to make the film the day I met Frank Serpico," recalls Al Pacino. "There was no script at that time and no director — Sidney Lumet came in later — but the moment I looked into that guy's eyes I knew I wanted to do it."[73] *Serpico*, based on Peter Maas' best-selling biography, follows the frustrations of police officer Frank Serpico from 1960 to 1971. The film focuses on how an honest New York City cop first refuses to acknowledge, then reports and finally exposes the rampant corruption which is seemingly entrenched in the system. The film also explores the loss of innocence of the young idealist as he resists that system. Within the framework of his professional anxiety, we experience his growing and destructive loneliness, alienation and paranoia.

John G. Avildsen was the original director of *Serpico*. Lumet took over the project on short notice after Avildsen left because of a dispute with Dino De Laurentice over the building of a set. After Lumet assumed responsibility, it was dispatched with his customary efficiency. *Serpico* was shot entirely on location in New York in fifty-one days (four days ahead of schedule). Included in the complex script were a hundred and seven different locations around the city and more than a hundred speaking parts. According to executive producer Roger Rothstein, "There were a couple of days when we did 34, 35 set-ups a day, and I just want to tell you — 35 set-ups in a nine-hour day is just fantastic!" [52].

Shooting was further complicated because as the film progresses Serpico goes from clean-faced to moustached to full-bearded, thus requiring that the film be shot in reverse chronological order. Not only was the order a problem, but the sets and props had to be painstakingly accurate to depict the subtle but important differences in, for example, car models during the eleven years that the film covers. Since it was all shot in fair weather, all the winter scenes had to be carefully staged, which included defoliating trees and simulating snow and visible breath.

When the film was released, practically everyone immediately thought it to be a very powerful and important statement, solidly directed, with a "brilliant" performance by Al Pacino. Most of the adverse criticism was aimed at the lack of a clearly delineated motivation for Serpico's intractable honesty. Andrew Sarris, writing in the *Village Voice,* noticed that "The trouble is that the screen Serpico is so completely isolated from everyone around him that it becomes difficult to determine how and why he evolved as he did."[74] Jay Cocks in *Time* magazine questioned the logic of his character: "It is clearly shown that Serpico is a New York street kid, but this movie asks us to accept that a man with that background could be aghast over a cop's getting free meals at a restaurant. . . ."[75]

Taking a perceptive interest in Lumet's progress at this critical period, Win Sharples, Jr., writing in *Filmmakers Newsletter,* argued the case for Lumet's development as a director. "What is surprising for Lumet is the overall sense of a unifying control, a sureness of creative purpose that marks this film as the finest work of its director's career. There has long been a nagging doubt that Lumet's notable talents — a permissive encourager of performance rather than an authoritative molder, an inspiring rather than inspired director — were enough to pull together a completely satisfying work . . ." [52].

Lumet himself said, "I'm thrilled. I'm not one to be cool about a hit, having had so many flops. I know the market place, and I know you need hits to survive in it" [51].

Lovin' Molly is a distinct departure from Lumet's usual fare. Instead of being an intense or controversial statement (like *Serpico*), *Lovin' Molly* is leisurely, quiet, pastoral and romantic. It is based on Larry McMurtry's novel *Leaving Cheyenne*, which follows the lives of three characters for forty years. Unlike McMurtry's two previous filmed books — *Hud* and *The Last Picture Show* — the weaknesses of the story overpowers its novelty and sincerity. The film played only a short while in theatres and was quickly sold to television.

The few critics who bothered to see and review the film typically compared it (unfavorably) to Truffaut's *Jules et Jim*, because both films covered a period of years in a triangular relationship between one magnetic woman and two magnetized men. Both women are literary earth-mother figures, radiating sensuality but oblivious to the pain they cause others. Kenneth Robinson of the *Spectator* mused that "The most remarkable thing about the story, in these permissive days, is the emphasis on the wages of sin."[76]

Murder on the Orient Express was made in England at a time when the British film industry was in serious trouble. It was the most ambitious and expensive British production in years, and it was hoped that the film would stimulate and revitalize the sagging industry. Like *Lovin' Molly*, this film was also a departure from Lumet's usual concerns. Lumet made *Murder on the Orient Express* as a deliberately and delicately glossy throwback to the thirties, highly stylized in an opulent fashion with a glamorous cast. From the opening credits, which are overlaid on crushed satin, it is clear that the film is a loving tribute to the classical detective story.

"The idea of having a cast full of stars," Lumet told Gordon Gow in an interview for *Films and Filming*, "was mine. This wasn't a thriller, it was a whodunnit and therefore old-fashioned. . . . I needed the stars. The byword became, 'Let's do a thirties movie; but if reality gets in the way, then to hell with reality' " [53]. In another interview with Quentin Falk in *Cinema-TV Digest*, Lumet revealed that "The stars in 'Express' were chosen for a very simple reason. The story takes place on a train that is snowbound. A train is a very limited visual experience so something better keep you bloody interested."[77]

Virtually everyone, critics and public alike, applauded the film. Lumet also liked the result because it solved a dilemma that had troubled him since *Bye, Bye Braverman*. "I've had a big problem that I've been aware of for years in my own work: a certain lack of charm. There's a kind of lightness that's extremely difficult to achieve. . . . Of course, I'm primarily a dramatic director and I think I'll always remain so, but what I'm talking about is a degree of colour that is terribly necessary just to have as a way of, among other things, offsetting drama. So immediately when I read Paul Dehn's script for *Murder on the Orient Express* I knew that from a style point of view it was something I'd been trying desperately to achieve. I mean when I did *Bye, Bye Braverman* I really messed it up" [53].

"It's an extraordinary story," commented Lumet about *Dog Day Afternoon*.

"In 1972 there was a bank robbery in New York which was a total mess. . . . True story. Insanely funny, terribly sad" [53]. The original screenplay by Frank Pierson, who wrote *The Anderson Tapes*, about an actual incident that occurred three years earlier, concerns three would-be robbers who blunder an attempt to rob a Brooklyn branch bank. The amateurishness of the robbers at first appears comic and then tragic, a comedy of errors that becomes a tragedy of contemporary life. The kind of dark humor presented in the film reflects the humor attempted in *Bye, Bye Braverman*.

Critical opinion was again sharply divided. *Rolling Stone* critic Jon Landau, calling the film "a bore," expressed the minority view: "It fails on all levels, especially in its construction. The picture remains throughout a vehicle in search of an idea. Everything suffers from lack of development."[78] Vincent Canby of the *New York Times* voiced the majority opinion by calling it "the best film he's [Lumet] ever made, with the exception of 'Long Day's Journey Into Night'. . . . [It is] full of thoughts, feelings and questions about the quality of a certain kind of urban civilization." And, as if in direct rebuttal to Landau's claim, Canby states, "It is a movie that knows what it's up to even when it's being ambiguous."[79]

In 1957, the year Lumet made *Twelve Angry Men*, Elia Kazan's *A Face in the Crowd* was the first film to directly confront the potential abuse of power in the television industry. It is a scathing view of the operations and politics of a local television station, depicting the medium as an irresponsible and manipulative force through which an unscrupulous opportunist is escalated into a demagogue. The subject of television was to lie virtually dormant for the next twenty years.

Network is a film that shouts. "It is dramatic dynamite," wrote the reviewer for *Playboy*, "a far-out fantasy that speaks to the Seventies the way *Dr. Strangelove* spoke to the chaotic Sixties more than a decade ago." Of Lumet's direction, the reviewer comments that he "dares a lot more than usual and emerges with upgraded credentials as a major American film maker, as audacious as Kubrick or Altman."[80] The film directly confronts the heated public controversy in recent years about the growing detrimental effect of television. It is both appropriate and ironic that writer Chayefsky, producer Howard Gottfried, and director Lumet all had their early experiences with television. *Network* was made twenty years after their association with television and seems to echo their collective concern about the regretful and wasteful direction television has taken in the years since they helped to make the Golden Age shine.

Network aims a series of harsh invectives against the medium that most powerfully touches all our lives, and an equally harsh indictment against a complicit public that passively responds to the maniacal manipulation. It defines a nightmare world of power-hungry big business, where insanity becomes prophesy, where divinity becomes commodity, where ratings and shares are traded for conscience and independence.

To those who accuse Chayevsky and Lumet of biting the hand that fed them, Lumet responds with a mixture of pride and concern: "The fact that it was about television would come very naturally from two people who had spent their creative youth in it. It was something we knew well. It was something nobody could lie to us about. Everybody keeps talking about the brilliant satiric nature of *Network*. To Paddy and me it wasn't satire at all, it was sheer reportage. Everything that you saw in *Network* had happened to either Paddy or myself — except for the actual shooting of Howard Beale on the air, and let's just give that a couple of more years. That is not out of the realm of possibility. It was not to us a diatribe against television. *Network* is about one very simple thing: the individual is getting lost as the mass becomes more and more identified with itself as a mass. And there is no greater epitomization of that than television."

After his blockbusting successes with *Serpico, Murder on the Orient Express, Dog Day Afternoon* and *Network,* Lumet returned to one of his central preoccupations: adapting stage plays to film. *Equus* playwright Peter Shaffer claims, "I tried [in the play] to create a mental world in which the deed could be made comprehensible." As in his previous ventures in filming plays, Lumet again decided for realism by "opening up" the stylized stagecraft to specific filmcraft; Shaffer's mental world becomes Lumet's real world. Reminiscent of the controversy attached to *Long Day's Journey into Night,* Lumet's filming of *Equus* immediately renewed the old debate about the nature of adapting plays to film. David Robinson stated categorically in the London *Times* that *"Equus* plays better on the screen than in the theatre,"[82] while Frank Rich of *Time* magazine argued that "If ever there was a play that has no business being a movie, *Equus* is it."[83]

One of the most celebrated and successful dramas of the seventies, *Equus* concerns a stableboy's passionate but uncomprehended crime (blinding six horses) and a psychiatrist's attempt to cure that passion. In resolving the case, the play becomes a modern Apollo-Dionysus dialectic: Is madness (the boy) actually a healthier virtue than sanity (the psychiatrist) in a society where mediocrity and safety are the inflexible molds? The boy is a disturbed youth in whom the religious and sexual fears instilled in him by his socially repressed parents have been diverted into a confused but fulfilling religio-sexual equestrian ecstasy. The provincial menopausal psychiatrist is forced to face the dilemma between his professional capacity to "cure" the boy of his pain (i.e., to scourge his psyche), and his humanitarian reluctance to neutralize the boy's intensity of feeling (i.e., "the power to worship"). In his personal life, the psychiatrist actually comes to envy the aberrant but expressed passion in his patient and to despise the impotence of his own unrealized passions.

The Wiz, Lumet's latest project, again is a play to be filmed. Unlike any of his previous films, however, *The Wiz* is a musical, a black hip version of *The Wizard of Oz,* and a spectacle, budgeted at some $20 million. But like so many of his other films, *The Wiz* is about New York City — Dorothy's escapades in Oz take her to such places as Harlem, the New York Public Library, the World Trade Center, the East River, and many other familiar New York sites.

The Wiz was originally to have been directed by John Badham, who left the project when Diana Ross was signed to play the role of Dorothy; Badham felt she was too old for the part of the teenage farmgirl. Coincidentally, it's being made at the old Paramount Astoria Studios on Long Island, where, in 1939, Lumet had acted in *One Third of a Nation*. "We hope to re-establish Astoria as a vital part of moviemaking in New York," Lumet speculates.[84]

In a 1968 interview in the *New York Times,* Lumet summarized his life's ambition: "When I'm 84, I'd like to see 60 pictures behind me. If only two of those are great pictures, I'll be a great man."[85] Although said rather facetiously, it certainly may be a realistic vision. Now at 54, with twenty-six films behind him and a healthy future ahead of him, it may well happen.

NOTES

1. John Crosby. *New York Herald Tribune* (4 November 1964).
2. Elizabeth Trotta. "Director Lumet at Work." *Newsday* (7 May 1963).
3. Stephen Watts. *New York Times* (15 May 1966), sec. II.
4. Sidney Lumet. "What Directors Are Saying." *Action*, 4 (November/December, 1969).
5. Sidney Lumet. Quoted in publicity release for *The Appointment* (1969).
6. Sidney Lumet. Quoted in interview with Rex Reed, *New York Times* (8 June 1968), sec. II.
7. Sean Connery. Quoted in *Screen* (4 December 1970).
8. Simone Signoret. Quoted in *London Times* (8 August 1968).
9. Robert Hooks. Quoted in interview with Rex Reed, *New York Times* (8 June 1969), sec. II.
10. James Coburn. Quoted in interview with Rex Reed, *New York Times* (8 June 1969), sec. II.
11. George Segal. Quoted in *New York Times* (23 April 1967), sec. II.
12. Sidney Lumet. Quoted by Barry Norman, *London Times* (19 March 1974).
13. Sidney Lumet. Quoted in *New York Times* (23 April 1967), sec. II.
14. Sidney Lumet. Quoted in *New York Times* (20 January 1974), sec. D.
15. Sidney Lumet. Quoted by Stephen Watts, *New York Times* (15 May 1966), sec. II.
16. Sidney Lumet. Quoted in *New York Times* (8 June 1968), sec. II.
17. Sidney Lumet. Quoted in publicity release for *The Appointment* (1969).
18. Sidney Lumet. Quoted in *New York Times* (20 January 1974), sec. D.
19. Sidney Lumet. Quoted in *New York Times* (20 January 1974), sec. D.
20. Sidney Lumet. Quoted in interview, *London Times* (19 March 1974).
21. John Coughlin. *Motion Picture Herald* (18 February 1939).
22. Frank Nugent. *New York Times* (19 February 1939), sec. X.
23. Sidney Lumet. Quoted in interview, *London Times* (3 March 1974).

Biographical Background / 33

24. Sidney Lumet. Quoted in *New York Times* (20 January 1974), sec. D.
25. Brooks Atkinson. *New York Times* (26 May 1948).
26. Erik Barnouw. *Tube of Plenty* (New York: Oxford, 1975).
27. Worthington Miner. Quoted by Max Wilk, *The Golden Age of Television* (New York: Delacorte, 1976).
28. Erik Barnouw. *Tube of Plenty* (New York: Oxford, 1975).
29. Sidney Lumet. Quoted in *New York Journal American* (14 February 1966).
30. William Hawkins. *New York World-Telegram* (12 January 1955).
31. Walter Kerr. *New York Herald Tribune* (12 January 1955).
32. Paddy Chayefsky. Quoted by Penelope Houston, "The Real Right Thing." *International Film Annual No. 2*, edited by William Whitebait (London: John Calder, 1958).
33. Tony Richardson. *Sight and Sound* (Autumn 1956).
34. Sidney Lumet. Quoted in *New York Times* (20 January 1974), sec. D.
35. Sidney Lumet. Quoted in *New York Times* (8 May 1960), sec II.
36. Sidney Lumet. Quoted in interview, *New York Times* (8 May 1960), sec. II.
37. Maurice Yacowar, *Tennessee Williams and Film* (New York: Ungar, 1977).
38. Boris Kaufman. Quoted by Frederick Foster, *American Cinematographer*, 41 (June 1960).
39. Sidney Lumet. Quoted in interview with Rex Reed, *New York Times* (8 June 1968), sec. II.
40. Derek Hill. *London Tribune* (9 September 1960).
41. Frank Aston. *New York World-Telegram* (17 February 1960).
42. Sidney Lumet. Quoted in interview with John Shanley, *New York Times* (7 August 1960), sec. II.
43. Isabel Quigly. *Spectator* (23 February 1962).
44. Sidney Lumet. Quoted in interview with Elizabeth Trotta, *Newsday* (7 May 1963).
45. Mary McCarthy. Quoted in *London Observer* (27 February 1966).
46. Sidney Lumet. Quoted in *London Observer* (27 February 1966).
47. Penelope Gilliatt. *London Sunday Observer* (25 September 1966).
48. Sidney Lumet. Quoted in *Variety* (1 February 1967).
49. Sidney Lumet. Quoted in *New York Times* (15 May 1966), sec. II.
50. Freddie Young. *American Cinematographer*, 47 (August 1966).
51. Richard Roud. *The Guardian* (3 February 1967).
52. Sidney Lumet. Quoted in *New York Times* (23 April 1967), sec. II.
53. Sidney Lumet. Quoted in *New York Times* (23 April 1967), sec. II.
54. Sidney Lumet. Quoted in *New York Times* (8 June 1968), sec. II.
55. Hollis Alpert. *Saturday Review* (25 January 1969).
56. Anon. *Time* (3 January 1969).
57. Peter Cowie. *50 Major Film-Makers* (London: Tantivy, 1975).
58. Margaret Hinxman. *London Sunday Telegraph* (21 December 1969).
59. Sidney Lumet. Quoted in publicity release for *The Appointment* (1969).
60. "Hawk." *Variety* (28 May 1969).
61. Rex Reed. *New York Times* (8 June 1969), sec. II.
62. Maurice Yacowar. *Tennessee Williams and Film* (New York: Ungar, 1977).

63. Anon. *Time* (19 January 1970).
64. Tennessee Williams. Quoted by Rex Reed, *People Are Crazy Here* (New York: Dell, 1975).
65. Maurice Yacowar. *Tennessee Williams and Film* (New York: Ungar, 1977).
66. Sidney Lumet. Quoted in *Variety* (1 January 1970).
67. Anon. *Variety* (28 July 1971).
68. John Russell Taylor. *London Times* (17 December 1971).
69. Andrew Sarris. *Village Voice* (22 July 1971).
70. Michael McKegney. *Village Voice* (4 January 1973).
71. Richard Schickel. *Time* (4 June 1973).
72. Margaret Hinxman. *London Sunday Telegraph* (1 January 1973).
73. Al Pacino. Quoted in *London Evening Standard* (29 March 1974).
74. Andrew Sarris. *Village Voice* (13 December 1973).
75. Jay Cocks. *Time* (31 December 1973).
76. Kenneth Robinson. *Spectator* (4 October 1975).
77. Sidney Lumet. Quoted in interview with Quentin Falk, *Cinema-TV Digest* (18 May 1974).
78. Jon Landau. *Rolling Stone* (23 October 1975).
79. Vincent Canby. *New York Times* (28 September 1975).
80. Anon. *Playboy* (December 1976).
81. Peter Shaffer. Quoted by David Robinson, *London Times* (21 October 1977).
82. David Robinson. *London Times* (21 October 1977).
83. Frank Rich. *Time* (31 October 1977).
84. Sidney Lumet. Quoted in *Screen International* (3 December 1977).
85. Sidney Lumet. Quoted in interview, *New York Times* (8 June 1968).

Critical Survey of Oeuvre

From his auspicious beginning with *Twelve Angry Men* to the controversial maturity of *Equus*, Sidney Lumet's career as a film director has oscillated between hits and misses. While many of his films were commercial giants, winning honors and tributes, many others were dwarfs, receiving only scant distribution and attention. Despite the notable inconsistencies of his commercial success, there is a marked consistency in his themes and characters. He does, upon close inspection, have manifest preoccupations in his work. Lumet seems to be at his dramatic best when studying men who are caught in the tense struggle of contemporary issues and weakest when the characters are allowed to control the issues.

For such a successful director, surprisingly little systematic exploration of his films has been made. Two abbreviated attempts to identify — rather than evaluate — subjects and themes in Lumet's body of films come from Peter Cowie and Maurice Yacowar. Cowie, in his *50 Major Filmmakers*, focuses on two themes. He suggests that Lumet tends, first, to exalt the individual who dares (usually on the basis of instinct rather than evidence) to stand up against the group and, second, to explore a person's loss of feeling which "is the most tragic aspect of Lumet's universe" [54]. Yacowar, in *Tennessee Williams and Film*, observes "two characteristically Lumet themes": first, Lumet's attraction to works about characters who cannot transcend their egotism, and second, Lumet's protagonists, who struggle to escape their past to create a new life.[1] Yet both Cowie and Yacowar treat Lumet only as one filmmaker among many. There has yet to be a thorough investigation of his films.

In a 1973 interview with Susan Merrill for *Films in Review*, Lumet was asked, "Do you feel that you've actually communicated any kind of idea in your films, any view of mankind or of the psyche that you've wanted to explore?" Lumet's reply is interesting. "I'd be terrified to get into it. I think there is too much articulation about the meaning of movies today" [49]. In a 1978 interview with the author, Lumet was asked to comment on his selection of material with respect to themes and characterizations. "I don't know about thematic lines in my work," he answered. "I was very interested in your outline — that you saw so many consistencies — and was rather delighted because for myself, I do not think about that, and yet I know that for work to be good that should be there. But I do not consciously make those selections. I trust the unconscious there totally. I figure if I trust the unconscious, the unconscious will come through."

Several issues that warrant attention in any critical survey of Lumet's films have already been discussed in the biographical chapter. Obviously his background in the theatre (acting) and in television (directing) have had a major impact on his selection of material and choice of techniques. Lumet's Yiddish origins have also found their way into his works, explicitly in *Bye, Bye Braverman* and *The Pawnbroker* and implicitly in many others. With only a few exceptions, another fascination for Lumet has been a marked affinity for realism, turning, for example, the mythic play *Orpheus Descending* and the abstract drama *Equus* into more credible and graphic statements.

LUMET'S SUBJECTS AND THEMES

Lumet works almost entirely from established material. He has adapted nine novels (*Fail Safe, The Pawnbroker, The Group, The Deadly Affair, Bye, Bye Braverman, The Anderson Tapes, Serpico, Lovin' Molly* and *Murder on the Orient Express*), but is better known for his many and often controversial adaptations of theatrical plays. "Obviously," he related to the author, "one of the reasons I began doing so many films of plays is because my whole heritage as a child was so involved with the theatre. Using plays as a source of material would fall naturally to me." Lumet's stage adaptations include five of his first six films (*Twelve Angry Men*, a teleplay, *Stage Struck, The Fugitive Kind, A View from the Bridge* and *Long Day's Journey into Night*) and fully half of his total film projects (the rest include *The Hill, The Sea Gull, Last of the Mobile Hot-Shots, Child's Play, The Offence, Equus* and the forthcoming *The Wiz*).

Lumet has been unusually articulate about his ideas on adapting stage plays to film, especially since he — probably more than any other contemporary director — has been so prolific in this area and has received so much attention for it. The process is dangerous, obviously, because of the tendency of critics to judge the film by the standards of the play. "In making them into films," Lumet told the author, "the primary thing is not to 'open it up.' To me, most critics have a very confused concept of cinema — they really are talking about scenery. I'm much more interested in a face than a mountain. For some people, if it's outdoor and against a tree and there are cattle around, it's a movie; but if it's against a piece of wallpaper with just a face in front of it, then it's a photographed stage play. That logic is nonsense. What makes it a movie instead of a photographed stage play is the use of *movie* techniques — camera, lighting, editing, sound, music — to make a statement that *only* the film itself can make: make a statement about the people, about the play."

Nearly all of Lumet's films deal with contemporary situations, especially group relationships and social comment. Of all his twenty-four completed films to date, only *The Group* and *Murder on the Orient Express*, both of which are set in the thirties, can be called period pieces. *Lovin' Molly* is a period piece only in its chronological structure; its theme relates more to the present than the past. To a lesser extent, *Long Day's Journey into Night* and *The Sea Gull*, both placed in the past, are period representatives; yet here also the relationships are timeless with only the dress, decor and styling indicating a past time.

Certainly more than any other director, Lumet has specialized in exploring profoundly the various facets of the city in which he has spent his life. Of his films, all but nine were either totally or in significant part filmed in New York. Of those filmed in the city, many were actually shot on the streets: *Stage Struck* (Broadway), *A View from the Bridge, Bye, Bye Braverman, Dog Day Afternoon* (all in Brooklyn), *The Pawnbroker* (Spanish Harlem), *The Anderson Tapes, Serpico* and *The Wiz* (all in Manhattan). Lumet has consistently demonstrated what the *Playboy* reviewer of *Dog Day Afternoon* hailed as his "intuitive grasp of the New York scene"[2] and what Alexander Walker in his review of the same film recognized as his knowledge of the city "like a patrolman on a lifetime's beat."[3] John Simon in his review of *Serpico* for *Esquire* praised Lumet because he "brings to the film a love-hate for the city that makes it so real that you shudder with affectionate loathing as the screen conveys the megalopolitan odors and grime directly to the respective centers in your brain."[4]

Most of Lumet's films center around a violent crime. The range of crimes is extraordinary: the question of guilt in a murder incident in *Twelve Angry Men*; ritualized murder in *The Fugitive Kind, Murder on the Orient Express* and *Network*; espionage and murder in *The Deadly Affair*; robbery and death in *The Pawnbroker, The Anderson Tapes* and *Dog Day Afternoon*; brutality and death in *The Hill* and *The Offence*; suicide in *A View from the Bridge, The Sea Gull, Child's Play* and *The Appointment*; maiming in *Child's Play* and *Equus*; child molestation and death in *The Offence*; corruption, graft and attempted murder in *Serpico*. Death also appears as a prominent factor in *Fail Safe, The Group, Bye, Bye Braverman* and *Last of the Mobile Hot-Shots*.

The "typical" Lumet situation revolves around an unusual event, typically a crime, which brings together a diverse group of people. The group must follow through with the consequences of that event to a resolution. *Fail Safe* begins with short vignettes of four unrelated people in four separate locations, all of whom will soon be intrinsically bound together in a desperate confrontation that may thrust the world into a nuclear holocaust. *Bye, Bye Braverman* takes four friends who are in pursuit of the funeral of a suddenly deceased friend; they spend the entire day together, although they never do arrive at the funeral — the correct funeral, that is. Both *Twelve*

Angry Men and *Murder on the Orient Express* are explications of murders; in the former, twelve jurors are brought together to consider the fate of a boy accused of murder, and in the latter twelve passengers are investigated for complicity in a revenge murder. *The Hill* portrays a cell of prisoners and their guards, locked in a struggle for self-respect and self-preservation. *The Anderson Tapes* and *Dog Day Afternoon* involve an attempted robbery and the consequent efforts of the robbers to complete the caper and of the police to foil their attempt. *Long Day's Journey into Night*, *The Sea Gull* and *A View from the Bridge* all focus on the intricate and intense family relationships that build until a crisis threatens the unity of the family. *The Group* involves eight superficially intimate graduates of Vassar and their subsequent interactions over the next half decade. *Child's Play* investigates the results of a power struggle between the two strong-willed teachers in a private boys' boarding school. And *Network* studies the operations of the executives vying for top positions in national television programming.

The single most dominant thematic situation in Lumet's films concerns a lone man who must stand against a hostile group. The confrontation between the individual and the group is usually not sought, but imposed from outside, by chance, fate, opportunity. Davis is one of the jurors who *happens* to be selected and confined with the eleven others. Val's car *happens* to break down in the small Mississippi town. Joe Roberts was the Warrant Officer who *happened* to be in command to receive an order that ran counter to his conscience. Poirot, fortunately, *happens* to be on the Orient Express when the murder takes place. Both Duke Anderson and Sonny Wortzik plan their respective robberies with precision, but neither can anticipate the unexpected or unpredictable — a paraplegic-asthmatic child who *happens* to be a ham radio enthusiast and a local shopkeeper who *happens* to become suspicious. Occasionally the lone man converts the group (as in *Twelve Angry Men*), but more frequently he is either defeated (as in *Dog Day Afternoon* and very nearly in *Serpico*) or succumbs to the group (as in *Murder on the Orient Express*). Whether he converts, loses or succumbs is apparently immaterial for Lumet — more important is whether he has acted in accord with his conscience.

Lumet's first feature, *Twelve Angry Men*, is a clear example of the lone man struggling against a hostile group. We know very little personal information about Juror Number Eight (Henry Fonda). We first see him as he rises with the others to leave the jury box in the courtroom and as they proceed to the jury room to begin their deliberations. There is nothing particularly outstanding or distinguishing about the man; he is simply one of many.

We are later provided with some pieces of personal data about him. At the end, for instance, we discover that he is an architect and his name is Davis. During the arguments, he is called a "do gooder" with a "soft sell" by Juror Number Seven (Jack Warden), who is only anxious to get the ordeal over so he can attend a ball game. At the end, Davis even has the forgiveness and compassion, despite others' verbal abuse, to assist the most recalcitrant of the group, Juror Number Three (Lee J. Cobb), who is now nearly broken by the truth.

Davis is, like many Lumet heroes, a common man who is placed in a position where he must come to terms with his conscience. The opening random comments and small talk among the jurors after the six-day trial give every indication that there *seems* to be no doubt about the boy's guilt. When the first vote is taken, only Davis dissents. Everyone else is thoroughly convinced of the verdict. Davis's position is not that the boy is innocent, but that "it's *possible*" that there exists a "reasonable doubt." He tells the others, with obvious reluctance and uncertainty, "I don't know. . . . I just want to talk. . . . It's not easy to raise my hand and send a boy off to his death without talking about it." The day is hot, the room is small, and tempers flare. But, as with many other Lumet heroes, Davis takes a risk. He calls for a secret ballot on the condition that if no one else votes "not guilty" he will then change his vote "guilty." The risk succeeds when Juror Number Nine (Joseph Sweeney) also wants "to hear more." Gradually, others are won over as it becomes clear that, indeed, there is a "reasonable doubt" about the defendant's guilt. By the fifth ballot, nine of the jurors are converted. Davis, now in a position of strength and confidence, tells the remaining holdouts (E. G. Marshall, Ed Begley and Lee J. Cobb), "We nine can't understand why you three are still *so* sure." And, shortly, the jury is unanimous in favor of acquittal.

Davis — like Joe Roberts, Charles Dobbs and Frank Serpico after him — is a man of conscience. It would have been the easiest and most obvious course of action to simply accept the surface evidence and concur with the logical conclusion. Davis, however, bases his dissent not on any tangible evidence but on intuition — on what he refers to as "possibilities" and "guesses." "*Nothing* is *that* positive," he admonishes the others about their "guilty" votes in the beginning. Justice prevails in *Twelve Angry Men*, not because of the courtroom arguments, but because one man has the courage to stand against the pressures of a group.

Another man who emerges from the crowd to distinguish himself is Charles Dobbs, an Intelligence Agent for the British government, in *The Deadly Affair*. Dobbs, like Davis, is hardly an exceptional man; he has been a dedicated agent since the War and has a fairly comfortable position. After Dobbs has investigated and exonerated a colleague who had been denounced as a communist, the man is found dead with a suicide note. Having interviewed him the day before, Dobbs cannot accept the "official" pronouncement of suicide. When ordered to close the case, Dobbs resigns to rectify the injustice he feels has been committed rather than accept a convenient but suspect decision. In pursuing the truth, he deliberately (and perhaps even self-destructively) exposes himself to both official censure and physical danger. Truth is served and a clever network of espionage and spying is broken because Dobbs refused to compromise, even though it meant the possible collapse of his marriage and death of his closest friends.

Perhaps the bleakest and most unrelenting statement of the lone individual against the group appears in *Serpico*. The film is concerned not so much with Serpico as a police officer combatting crime in the "underworld" (we only see fragments of this activity) as with a man of conscience confronting the conscienceless and expansive practice of corruption *within* "the system."

The film begins with Serpico lying on the stretcher in a squad car. He has been shot in the face, and a barely audible voice in the background asks, "Did a cop do it?" Almost immediately we are taken back eleven years to the time when a clean shaven and neatly dressed Frank Serpico, fresh from the Police Academy, listens with idealism to the optimistic words of the officer giving the commencement address. On his first assignment as a uniformed patrolman, he begins to witness the harmless but noticeable territoriality of his senior partner, who advises against responding to a distress call ("Relax Frank, it's not our sector"), and the obvious negligence in a theft apprehension ("It's Muscle's case. It'll keep").

After a few years on the force, when assigned to plain-clothes street duty, Serpico begins to confront the big payoffs. He refuses all graft offers, and the internal pressures quickly mount. Other cops consider him a threat to their security, since most consider payoffs simply a fringe benefit of the job. "It's incredible," he complains in one of his tirades. "I feel like a criminal because I don't take money." He begins to tape phone conversations and to suspect everyone. In desperation, he goes to his first "outside agency" (the Mayor's Office), but the Mayor prefers to disregard his evidence. He becomes increasingly paranoid and singularly disagreeable, obsessed by wanting to be left alone to do his job as a cop. With increasing frequency, he rails to whomever will listen, gradually driving friends and lovers away from him. Serpico becomes an oddity: a cop who is more hated and threatened by his police colleagues than by his criminal adversaries. His solitary honesty is seen as an aberration in a system where corruption has become the standard. When all seems at a precarious and futile impasse, he complains to his superiors, "I'm a marked man in this department, and for what?"

For what, indeed? The viewer is left with the impression that virtually everyone on all levels of the New York police force — from the well-meaning patrolman who accepts the free lunches, to the narcotics detectives who consider the usual payoff money mere "chicken feed", to perhaps even the Mayor who considers it inadvisable to investigate the corruption — is "on the take" and accepts it as routine. It is highly ironic, seen from the outside, when one cop within the system can genuinely ask, "Who can trust a cop that don't take money?" They all have families and interests to protect, and most are presented as otherwise everyday men. Serpico's persistence eventually results in the Knapp Commission hearings, which opened up the scandalous and rampant corruption in the police department.

One of the most vivid examples of the single man opposing the group occurs in *Dog Day Afternoon*. What appears for a moment to be a well planned and executed bank robbery quickly becomes a travesty. Stevie gets "bad vibes" and leaves, the money is picked up instead of delivered, the smoke from the burning bank records is seen by a curious neighbor. Within fifteen minutes, two hundred and fifty cops arrive and cordon off the street, television crews set up their cameras and spectators crowd around the barricades.

Sonny, along with the slow-witted Sal and a dozen, mostly female hostages, are trapped inside the bank with the police outside. The police try to bargain and convince Sonny to surrender. It appears for a while to be a hopeless stalemate. When Sonny takes the offensive and begins making *his* demands, he becomes a momentary folk hero for the crowd because he actively resists the constricting forces of society. But Sonny's glory is short-lived.

Like Bonnie and Clyde, Sonny is not perceived as a criminal. Even though he is unquestionably involved in an illegal enterprise, he is not portrayed as a dangerous person. Like many other Lumet characters, he is presented as an "unfortunate" who is caught in a situation he did not want and cannot resolve. Since the audience's sympathies so strongly favor Sonny, society can be accused of complicity in not successfully integrating its eccentric but amicable element. Society, in one view, is depicted as compelled to destroy what it does not understand and refuses to assimilate. Again, as in many other Lumet narratives, events seem to dominate men, and people are caught in the consequences of events. No one wants the inevitable violence, but no one knows how to prevent it.

The most dominant theme in Lumet's films certainly concerns the lone man as he confronts and opposes the pressures of a hostile group. Although the single individual may be alone in his struggle, he has a dignity, courage and conviction that is admirable. His decisions may be questionable, but he gives the effort everything he has. Although he may not succeed in his struggle, the audience is usually with him. Questions of guilt or innocence, right or wrong, good or evil dissolve into rhetorical propositions. What emerges in Lumet's world is a peculiar kind of twentieth century nobility and heroism — the rare individual who dares to oppose the mob. Whether he is guilty or innocent, right or wrong, good or evil is academic. What becomes central for Lumet is that he takes the risk and assumes responsibility in an effort that can inspire both admiration and pathos.

Another theme of special prominence for Lumet, especially in his more recent films, is the deleterious effect of the media. Ever since Jeb and Myrtle, in *Last of the Mobile Hot-Shots*, were married on television (without even knowing each other's name) on the "Happy Couple Time" segment of *The Rube Benedict Show*, the media has been a prime target for Lumet's sense of irony.

In *The Anderson Tapes*, which immediately followed *Last of the Mobile Hot-Shots*, the media occupies an impressive if menacing position. "You've been inside ten years," a fellow inmate warns Duke Anderson the day he is released from prison. "It's a changed world." The world, indeed, has changed. Although Anderson seems unaware of it, we are not. The world of *The Anderson Tapes* is slowly, but surely, becoming a totalitarian environment where individual freedom is a mere illusion. Pop's well-intentioned compliment to Anderson about his image on the closed-circuit television system during the robbery — "Hey Duke, you look swell on the tv" — serves as an ironic commentary by the filmmaker. In *The Anderson Tapes*, the television media is used in two different but related ways, one exploring surveillance devices and the other news coverage.

According to the film, no one is spared the invasion of privacy by concealed surveillance equipment. Anderson is inadvertently recorded on various independent systems, because all those with whom he associates are being recorded: he's watched or taped in the prison, the bus station, the bank, the bedroom, local shops, elevator lifts, private homes, public cafes, moving cars — virtually everything he says or does is scrupulously monitored by concealed microphones, taps, bugs, cameras, earphones, recorders, transmitters.

Although Anderson's every move and word seem to be monitored, the irony is clear: no one is paying any attention specifically to *him*. The irony emerges since all the technological gadgets designed to invade privacy are so highly specialized as to be ultimately self-defeating, because there is no source to coordinate all the fragments. While Anderson believes that he is executing the caper of a lifetime in secrecy, the unseen and unheard world of peeping and eavesdropping is constantly observing and listening. The final irony is that none of the sophisticated devices interferes with the caper even though they all know about it; and equally ironic is the fact that Anderson's defeat is actually Angelo's salvation, since the tapes implicating him have to be erased.

During the flash-forwards that periodically interrupt the actual robbery, television newsmen are on the scene interviewing the various victims. This is done in the style which the media would actually use to cover and exploit the event, asking all the appropriate questions and showing the appropriate gore (noticeable in the backgrounds) and complete with the illusion of on-the-spot intimacy using hand-held equipment.

If the televised reportage of the aftermath of the robbery in *The Anderson*

Tapes is intended as imitation, then the media coverage of the robbery in *Dog Day Afternoon* is hardly less than tasteless and exploitative. The television crews and "live eye" camera facilities arrive with the police. Before long, what was (and probably should have remained) a minor incident becomes a major event. Sonny and the others inside the bank even watch the events as they happen on Mulvaney's small desk set. But perhaps the most effective jab at the television media occurs when a newsman has the audacity to attempt a live phone interview from the outside with Sonny, who is holed up inside the bank. After a few trivial questions, Sonny abruptly begins to bargain with the interviewer, in much the same way he has been bargaining with Moretti. "We're entertainment, right? Whata you got for us?" he asks. When Sonny, outraged, yells "fuck" to the newsman on the phone (the conversation is being broadcast), the television set on Mulvaney's desk quickly blurts out an apology for technical difficulties and then cuts to the Looney Tune theme music.

It is also through television that we are provided with the information about Sonny's homosexual marriage to Leon, which is editorially mocked by television. Sal becomes highly alarmed that he, too, was called a homosexual on the television, with its millions of anonymous viewers. Although Sal's entire future rests on the events of the next few hours, he becomes distressed over the thought that the viewers will regard him as a homosexual when he is not.

Sonny, certainly more than anyone else, correctly perceives the ruthless and hypocritical nature of media exploitation. To passify Sal's concern, for example, Sonny merely passes it off with the comment, "It's just a freak show to them anyway" — as if it would not make the slightest difference whether it were accurately reported or not. Sonny, in fact, takes full advantage of the "freak show" phenomenon and becomes, literally, a performer for both the crowd and the media. He becomes, for an instant, a celebrity.

Network, certainly the single most scathing indictment of the television media yet, was made some twenty years after Lumet and Chayevsky left television for films. Rather than portraying the surveillance or entertainment aspects of the media, the thrust of *Network* presents the business aspect of television. Max, in an indirect extension of Sonny's pejorative comments, calls the programmers "grave robbers" for viciously and callously exploiting Howard Beale's condition "like a carnival freak."

The television business in *Network* is depicted as a harrowing nightmare world, in which decisions are based on impersonal reports, projections, analyses and statistics. Television is used to manipulate a sheepish public, to reduce important issues to common banalities, to exploit the weaknesses and fears of viewers — all to the competitive advantage of corporate profits and personal ambitions. Television is perceived as controlled by a mercenary elite who have exchanged their souls for power. The business is ulcerous and precarious, where positions and fortunes are made and lost with overnight ratings and shares. Survival often depends on how well the corporate personalities can manipulate others while protecting themselves with the weapons of back-biting, back-fighting and back-stabbing. People and personalities are expendable commodities, to be exploited only as long as it is profitable and then to be discarded by any means available.

Perhaps the most direct assault on the television industry comes in Max's parting words to Diana: "You are one of Howard's humanoids, and if I stay with you, I'll be destroyed. Like Howard Beale was destroyed. Like everything you and the whole institution of television touch gets destroyed! You are indifferent to all suffering, insensitive to joy. All of life is reduced to the common rubble of banality. War, murder, death are all the same to you as bottles of beer. The daily business of life is a corrupt comedy. You even shatter sensations into jagged fragments of minutes, split-seconds and instant replays. You are madness incarnate, Diana, virulent madness, and whatever you touch dies with you. Well, not me! Not while I can still feel pleasure and pain and love!" Even though these are the final words of a departing lover, they seem to express many of the sentiments that form a disturbing and rather cynical core in Lumet's later films.

Perhaps because Lumet chooses subjects that place the individual against the forces of a group or an institution, his films typically end either in death or despair. Only his first three films can be said to have the traditional "happy ending"; justice, dedication and love triumph, respectively, in *Twelve Angry Men, Stage Struck* and *That Kind of Woman*. More often, however, Lumet's films tend to end tragically. *The Fugitive Kind, The Anderson Tapes, Child's Play* and *Network* each has the major protagonist(s) violently killed at the end. *The Pawnbroker, The Hill, The Offence, Serpico* and *Dog Day Afternoon* all leave the protagonist in a position of near hopelessness. *A View from the Bridge, The Sea Gull* and *The Appointment* each concludes with the suicide of a major character. *Fail Safe* climaxes with the destruction of both Moscow and New York City. Of the eight girls in *The Group*, only Polly (and perhaps Lakey) achieve a satisfactory love relationship. At their most optimistic, Lumet's films are left ambiguous. Perhaps the Tyrone family will find unity in *Long Day's Journey into Night*; perhaps Dobbs and his estranged wife will be reconciled in *The Deadly Affair*; and perhaps Myrtle and Chicken will find happiness in *Last of the Mobile Hot-Shots*. In both *Bye, Bye Braverman* and *Lovin' Molly* nothing is resolved, because there is nothing to resolve. *Murder on the Orient Express* is curious, because the detective sides with the criminal conspirators.

When asked about his lack of happy endings, Lumet told the author: "I've asked myself the same question. I'm not a dour person by nature. I enjoy life and pleasure and comfort. But obviously there is something in me that lets me know that there are no such things as happy endings. When I read a script with a happy ending, I tend not to believe the whole story."[5]

LUMET'S CHARACTERS

Lumet tends to concentrate on intensive male character studies. His characters are fraught with the complexities and contradictions of contemporary society. They are frequently strong willed men, able to manipulate and influence others. For example, Lumet deals with psychological manipulation and lethal games in *Child's Play*, with the search for salvation in *The Fugitive Kind*, with corruption in law enforcement in *Serpico*.

Lumet's heroes, therefore, tend to be isolated men struggling to resolve a desperate situation. Some of his characters struggle against the isolation created by their own past: Val in *The Fugitive Kind*, Nazerman in *The Pawnbroker*, Johnson in *The Offence*. Others, men of conscience, are isolated because they stand in opposition to injustice or destruction: "Davis" in *Twelve Angry Men*, the President in *Fail Safe*, Roberts in *The Hill*, Dobbs in *The Deadly Affair*, Serpico in *Serpico*, Poirot in *Murder on the Orient Express*. Still others are isolated because of their own peculiar sense of desperation: Federico in *The Appointment*, Sonny in *Dog Day Afternoon*, Dysart and Strang in *Equus*. As Val takes Lady's hand in his (it is the first time they touch), he tells her, "We're all confined to isolation inside our own skins. That's as close as we get to know each other — flesh." Lady angrily replies, "Not for me." Val's observation and Lady's response might well serve as a caption for many of the characters in Lumet's gallery, from Davis in *Twelve Angry Men* to Dysart in *Equus*.

Entrapped by their painful isolation, Lumet's protagonists are often unlikable and unpleasant men who are obsessed, who have allowed their professional lives to influence or even control their personal lives. Nazerman suffers from the binding guilt and resentment of a repressed past so powerful that he regards the rest of humanity as contemptuous "scum." Federico quietly and formally, perhaps even inadvertently, persecutes his wife into suicide by his insidious and compulsive suspicions. Johnson, like Nazerman, is a singularly bitter and hostile man driven into a psychotic condition by his years of investigating violent and grotesque crimes as a police detective. Serpico, also a police officer, is pushed into a tormented paranoia in which he comes to believe that corruption is the standard and everyone is a potential assassin.

Lumet's heroes exist on the fringes of both society and madness. They may be young or middle-aged, they may be active or passive, they may be settled or transient. They are all outsiders and they are all loners who are obsessed by some conviction or action. Burdened by their obsessions, they are, for the most part, disagreeable people. They have not been able to reconcile their pasts or beliefs with the world in which they must live and function.

One of the recurrent statements about human nature that permeates Lumet's films is the effect of memory on individuals who have attempted to escape from their pasts. A representative case, even though he is not a leading figure, is Colonel Cascio in *Fail Safe*. Cascio has his origins in the lower class, which he keeps hidden from his colleagues in the military. He has worked his way into a position of prominence and responsibility in the Air Force and feels only shame for his derelict father and ineffectual mother. When his background is inadvertently discovered by General Bogan, Cascio becomes noticeably uncomfortable and defensive in Bogan's company. Under the strain of divulging secret military information to the Soviets in an attempt to prevent the bombers in Group Six from reaching Moscow, Cascio breaks. Restrained and carried out of the command base, he shouts, presumably to Bogan, "I'm better than you are." Like so many Lumet figures, Cascio cannot, regardless of how hard he tries, escape his past.

The man who is perhaps most plagued and victimized by the repressed effects of his past upon the present is Sol Nazerman in *The Pawnbroker*. Nazerman, called "the living dead" by his mistress's father, suffers from a prolonged and unresolved guilt about surviving in the Nazi concentration camps. "I didn't die," he confesses as if it were a sin to have lived. Concealed behind a veneer of insensitivity, he treats everyone who enters his Harlem pawnshop with equal contempt: the old man who just wants to talk, the thieves with their stolen lawnmower, the dope addict with the worthless radio, the social worker who tries to solicit a contribution, the young pregnant girl who has been abandoned. They and their stories mean nothing to him. He hides from the world and himself behind the ominous wire mesh of his cage, both a physical and cerebral prison. He calls his customers "creatures" and questions what "right" they have even to be alive.

The Pawnbroker is Nazerman's psychological biography. Like Cascio, Nazerman also has a breaking point, which is reached when he discovers that the money he has made by cooperating with a Harlem racketeer had come from prostitution. The selling of bodies in Harlem is too reminiscent of the degradations forced upon the women, including his wife, in the camps. After this painful revelation, Nazerman is thrown into a spiritual upheaval and becomes dedicated to self-destruction. Reversing his usual callousness, he begins to give fifty dollars for gilded baby shoes and two dollars for a Likra camera. He abuses customers and alienates Ortiz. When Rodriquez appears at the pawnshop to have some papers signed, Nazerman refuses, expecting and hoping to be killed for his refusal. Rodriquez correctly senses that it would be a worse torture to let Nazerman live. When the gang of local hoodlums comes to rob the shop, Nazerman refuses them the money. Again expecting and hoping to be killed, he is spared only because Ortiz intercedes and intercepts the fatal bullet.

Nazerman survives Harlem just as he had survived the camps; just as he expresses guilt that he did not die in the camps, so he assumes a Christ-like guilt that he does not die in Harlem. His family died in the camps; Ortiz died in Harlem; he still survives.

Detective Sergeant Johnson in *The Offence* is yet another Lumet protagonist haunted by his past. For twenty years Johnson has constantly been investigating crimes of violence. The gradual, imperceptible cumulative effect of internalizing all these years has been to turn Johnson into the very same kind of maniac he has worked so intensely to eliminate. He is not able, as Cartwright tells him he must, to "Keep a part of you separate. . . . You've got to accept that you're two people: police officer and the bloak you are off duty."

Upon investigating and interrogating suspects in a series of child molestations, Johnson immediately decides that Baxter is the guilty man. His decision results not from evidence, but from an intuitive recognition that Baxter is tormented by guilt. Indeed, Baxter is tormented by guilt; but it is the guilt of realizing that, after eighteen years of marriage, he is a homosexual. Baxter also senses the guilt in Johnson: "Nothing I have done can be half as bad as the thoughts in your head. . . . I don't have to tell you anything — you know exactly what it's like. Nothing I can, you haven't imagined." Johnson mistakes and even shares Baxter's unresolved guilt, and he fatally beats Baxter because he perceives the guilt of his own psyche reflected in Baxter's words.

There is a strong implication that the man Johnson is hunting for child molesting could be Johnson himself. When Johnson finds the fourth victim, only he of all the searchers knows exactly where to find the missing child in the dense and dark woods. Upon finding her, the girl, still in shock, repels from him in fright. Having repressed so many images and perhaps incidents of violence, it takes Cartwright's insistent interrogation to bring Johnson to a recognition of what has happened to him and what he has become. "In God's holy name," Johnson uncontrollably utters, "all I can see are pictures in my mind. Clouded. Ten million bloody pictures. I tried to stop them, keep them somewhere in the dark at the back of my mind. They won't rest, leave me rest. All I can see, looking down, her body, whiteness, her white body, him, pushing himself, forcing himself, pressing down on her, tearing into her, screaming. I can see her hands. . . ." While this frenzied evocation is being vocalized by Johnson, the screen images are those of the child-victim's smiling and inviting face and his tender touch, all of which is toned with a soft yellow-orange. It is left unsettled whether Johnson is the child molester because the attention of the plot of *The Offence* shifts from "Who molested the children?" to "Why did Johnson beat Baxter?" What is perhaps more important, however, is the certainty of Johnson's capability of schizophrenic psychosis.

From *Twelve Angry Men* to *Equus*, Lumet has consistently explored pivotal characters, who, for a variety of personal and professional reasons, have been driven to the limit, who have become desperate men struggling to find a way out of the maze in which they find themselves trapped. His films have been populated by such characters, frequently at odds with their sense of conscience, commitment and identity.

Lumet's repertoire covers a wide range of characterizations, from the jurors who must decide the fate of the accused boy, to the President who must decide the course of future history, to Sol Nazerman who is forced out of his insulated barbedwire prison of memories, to Joe Roberts who is busted because he refused to obey a suicidal command, to Sergeant Johnson who is driven to murder by the effects of two decades of police service, to Frank Serpico who simply wants to be left alone to do his job, to Dr. Dysart who has reached a personal and professional crisis in which he must re-affirm or re-define his sense of identity. Whatever their motives or circumstances, all these characters share a common dilemma. They are all involved in desperate situations, the situation often directing the desperation.

Even among Lumet's supporting characters, there is a frequent recurrence of this desperation. In his first film, *Twelve Angry Men*, Juror Number Three (Lee J. Cobb) represents one such instance. At first he seems friendly enough and interested in serving the cause of justice. He tells a fellow juror that he operates the "Beck and Call" messenger service. He started from nothing and by hard work and sacrifice has made it into a profitable business.("Hit 'em where they live" is his pragmatic motto.) And, of the twelve jurors, he is the only one to have taken notes during the trial. Like the others, he assumes the boy's guilt.

As the deliberations proceed and as more of the jurors change from "guilty" to "not guilty," his veneer of composure and rationality disintegrates. With an increasingly emotional and abrasive attitude, he staunchly resists any suggestion or argument of the boy's possible innocence. He even tries to demonstrate, beyond reason, how the boy could have inflicted the fatal knife wound at an improbable angle of entry.

It becomes clear that he wants to persecute the boy for personal motives. We learn that his own son fought with him and left home two years earlier. It becomes apparent that the accused boy's insolence toward his father has reinforced Juror Number Three's belief that all youths are contemptuous. He is so despondent about his own son's lack of regard for him that he is willing, albeit unconsciously, to convict an innocent boy, a surrogate for his own son. Of the twelve, he is the last hold-out. To admit that the boy is innocent, even to himself, would be tantamount to admitting his own son might have been right. The defeat of having to acknowledge the boy's innocence is too much for him. When he finally changes his vote, he emotionally breaks down. "Rotten kids," he sighs, mostly to himself. "You work your heart out." He removes the snapshot of his son from his wallet and viciously tears it to pieces. His conviction about youth challenged, his sense of self-respect shaken, Juror Number Three will probably emerge a better person for the ordeal. Davis, in a gesture of support, helps him on with his jacket as they are about to leave the jury room.

Federico in *The Appointment* is another desperate man. Like Juror Number Three, he is deceived by a distorted logic that becomes an obsession. Federico's desperation resides in his unsettling suspicion that Carla, his wife, has been, and still is, an expensive and "truly exceptional" prostitute. It is, in fact, the thought of her as a prostitute that both excites and threatens Federico.

He first notices her on the street, then meets her as the fiancee of a colleague, and finally, when her engagement is broken off, pursues her for himself. But it is Carla's past that he cannot dispel from his mind. Rather than confront her directly, like one who cares, he seeks incriminating/acquitting evidence, like a lawyer: he secretly follows her, he catches her in a falsehood, he makes inquiries and attempts to arrange an "appointment" with the mysterious but unseen prostitute he believes to be Carla. He even tells her at one point, "Sometimes it seems terrible that you should have had a life before me." She answers, "Don't worry. I'm not going back to my job." This, of course, raises even more suspicions in Federico, since it is not clear whether she is referring to her former job as a model or, perhaps, to her job as a prostitute. Instead of trapping her, his obsession to expose her as the prostitute only succeeds in driving her to suicide. And then, with a bitter irony, Federico discovers that he has been pursuing an illusion — Carla was not the prostitute, but the loving and faithful wife he had wanted.

One of Lumet's most enigmatic characters is Joe Dobbs in *Child's Play*. He has taught English at St. Charles boarding school for boys for ten years. During that period he has held guardianship over the junior class and now aspires to the senior class position. But the senior class is the domain of Jerome ("Lash") Malley, the austere Latin teacher who was to retire after thirty years of teaching. To thwart Dobb's ambition, Malley has decided to remain at the school.

The animosity between the two rivals becomes so intense that it filters down to affect the behavior of "the boys." Brutality, torture, maiming begin to occur among the boys with alarming frequency. At first it seems that Dobbs is the benevolent force and Malley the malevolent force. By all appearances, Dobbs cares for his boys (with what Malley calls an abnormal paternalism), and Malley only seeks to punish them with demanding assignments. In fact, however, Dobbs has so manipulated the thoughts and attitudes of his junior boys that they enact his thoughts. Like an adept Pavlovian, Dobbs has skillfully directed the boys against Malley, rewarding them with his affection.

Dobbs feels himself pushed to this course because Malley has refused to retire. To protect what he believes to be a flagrant injustice, he maneuvers the boys into the sinister instruments of his own psyche. Although it is clear that Dobbs thoroughly believes that what he is doing is for the best, it is ambiguous how much he actually perceives of what he has done to himself and others. But in some mesmerizing way, he is the source of the evil that has infected St. Charles.

Serpico is another Lumet character who is so totally committed that it jeopardizes his own life. Early in the film, Serpico relates a childhood incident about how impressed he had been over the commanding presence of a policeman during a difficult situation. Since that time, he claims, he has always wanted to emulate that idealism. As a seasoned patrolman, however, Serpico finds himself caught in a world of graft, corruption and negligence in the institution he has admired since childhood. It is important to note that Serpico doesn't blame or judge others for taking the payoff money; he simply wants to be left alone, without harassment, to do his job (that is, presumably, to live up to his childhood image). It is only when he is threatened by his fellow officers, who feel that because he doesn't take payoffs he is not to be trusted, that he is forced to expose them for his own protection. Ironically, had the others ignored him it is likely that Serpico would have done nothing.

Although we can certainly applaud his principles and dedication, what is perhaps most curious and interesting about Serpico is the unspecified motivation for his conspicuous and uncompromising honesty. The anecdote about his adolescent hero-worship seems insubstantial to warrant his self-conscious and even self-rightous ethics. In one sense, it can certainly be argued that Serpico invites the persecution he receives. Whether his rigorous refusal to accept payoffs derives from a childhood idealism or a self-destructive fanaticism is unclear; what is clear, however, is that he could have avoided the ensuing persecution without compromising his ethics, had he been less outspoken and more discreet.

Certainly the pressures on Serpico are pressures that he as much creates for himself as they are created for him. Whether he realizes it or not, he is the one who places himself in peril. As a result of the desperation he creates, he turns against everyone with a paranoid hostility. He indulges in long and loud tirades to whoever will listen, gradually losing friends and those who would be his friends. As much as we can appreciate the strength of his incorruptibility, the film fails to resolve one perplexing thought: Serpico did have options. He drives himself into an hysterical desperation and, like so many other Lumet protagonists, he becomes a highly disagreeable and unpleasant man.

Dr. Martin Dysart in *Equus* is a prototypical Lumet character: a man caught in a desperate situation. He is a middle-aged psychiatrist who questions the validity of his own function. He seems to be more capable of helping others than himself. Dysart is a personally isolated and professionally frustrated man. He feels the emotional drain of his professional life and routinizes a distant, empty relationship with his wife. He dreams of the gods and landscape of ancient Greece. Filled with self-doubt and self-reproach, he makes an obsession of challenging his own worth. After first meeting Alan Strang, Dysart, in a soliloquy to the audience, relates the details of a dream he experienced; the dream recounts his own suppressed desire for god-like worship and ventures into excess.

Alan, the patient, is also a person driven to desperation by an unresolved personal dilemma. He finds something pure and dependable, something elemental and inexplicable in his affection for horses. Alan's adolescent attraction to horses goes beyond the socially acceptable. He internalizes it to the point at which he mimics their gestures and strides with his own body; he reveals how he experiences a sexual excitement for the feel of their coat, the powerful lines of their torso, their scent on the curry brush. Alan's passion is contrasted to the sterile relationships everyone in the adult world seems to exhibit. Alan is placed in the care of the psychiatrist because he has, without apparent motivation, violently blinded six horses.

Both Dysart and Alan are sexually aberrant. Dysart has become sexually inert, channeling all his energies into work; Alan is attempting to resolve his sexual confusion, sublimating his energy into a desire for horses. In this strange and somehow mutually fulfilling exchange, the needs of both doctor and patient gradually congeal. Alan has a passion of such intensity that it has brought him to an unbearable "pain"; but it is an intensity and pain that Dysart, because of his own stifled existence, comes to envy. Dysart says to his confidant, Hester, "I tell you that boy has known a passion more ferocious than I've known in my entire life. . . . He's saying 'I've galloped and you haven't.' I'm actually jealous of Alan Strang." He goes on to accuse himself of suffocating his own life, "and I go off to the hospital to treat *him* for insanity!" The boy desperately wants to rid himself of his affliction but doesn't know how. The psychiatrist desperately wants to feel the passionate surge that his patient has felt but doesn't know how. Alan's account of the incident activates the suppressed passions that Dysart has only dreamed about. "It asks questions I've avoided all my professional life," he confesses to Hester. Dysart suffers as much pain as Alan.

Dysart periodically faces and speaks directly to the audience from the desk in his office. He typically comments on the ineffectuality of his life or the pain of his patient. His final address, as the camera slowly moves in to a closeup, is revealing. "My achievement," he comments, "is more likely to make a ghost [of Alan]. . . . Passion, you see, can be destroyed by a doctor; it can't be created. You'll gallop no more Alan." Dysart is relieved because he has cured Alan's pain, but concurrently he is also saddened because he has neutralized the intensity; what replaces the pain and intensity is a harmless emptiness, like Dysart's own life. There is an element of self-accusation in his voice because he can't cure his own pain. "I stand in the dusk with a knife, wildly stabbing," he concludes with a sense of hopelessness. "I need more desperately than my children a way of seeing in the dark."

Lumet's world tends to be male dominated. His films are principally composed of a male group. His first film, *Twelve Angry Men*, has no women in the cast. *The Hill* and *Child's Play* have only a few women, and those are negligible roles. *Fail Safe, Bye, Bye Braverman, Serpico, Dog Day Afternoon,* and *Equus* all have women who only function as foils, supports or confidants for men.

Where women do have some importance, it is mostly weak or negative. They do not understand, nor can they share the lives of, their men. The heroine of *Stage Struck* is, like the women in *The Group*, dominated by men. She is exceptional as an acting talent but becomes a star performer only by the support and training of men. Lady in *The Fugitive Kind* is so strong-willed as to be self-destructive. Her blinding efforts to take revenge on the town and especially on her husband for the murder of her father take precedence over her regenerative love for Val. As a result, both are killed. The mother in *Long Day's Journey into Night*, although the center of the family, lives in past hopes and dreams. She is dependent upon her addiction to narcotics to sustain her failing life. Carla in *The Appointment* becomes an accessory in her own destruction by being so weak and passive. Rather than resisting Federico's persecution, she merely acquiesces and prefers suicide to confrontation. In *The Offence*, when Sergeant Johnson returns to his apartment after beating Baxter, he immediately verbally attacks his wife. Releasing his buried agonies and hostilities, he bitterly and abusively complains to her of his unhappy home life and her failure to understand him. In *The Anderson Tapes*, Ingrid Everleigh is a Park Avenue mistress. She is treated as a child by her bill-paying lover, Werner, who refers to her as a "four-bit hooker." Although Ingrid doesn't like Werner, she feels herself too weak to leave him, so she chooses Werner's security over Duke's affection. The two women in Serpico's life exist only, apparently, to be abused by his constant and obsessive railings.

There are a number of films in which women occupy the central position, such as *Lovin' Molly, Network* and *The Group*. They appear to be strong and determined women, yet on closer inspection these women fare no better than the others. The elaboration of their roles does not improve their lot.

In *Lovin' Molly*, Molly has the focal position in the lives of three men: Gid, Johnny and Eddie (who is seldom seen). Molly is, like Lara in *Dr. Zhivago*, an earth-mother figure. She is independent, resolute and sensual. As appealing as she is, she will have no other way but her own, without understanding and without compromising. Although she cloaks her egotism in proclamations of freedom (her word is "silliness"), she seems totally oblivious to the pain and suffering she causes others; Gid is repeatedly hurt by her, and one of her illegitimate sons hates her. Her free spirit may be argumentatively commendable, but it can also be socially destructive.

Diana Christensen in *Network* is perhaps the epitome of the career-obsessed woman whose work dominates her entire life. When she has dinner with Max, she appraises herself with an uncanny accuracy. "I seem to be inept at everything except my job. I'm very good at my job. All I want out of life is a 30 share and a 20 rating." (At the dinner, Max discusses his twenty-five years of marriage and his two daughters.) She is a dedicated professional: aggressive, exploitative, callous and opportunistic. She acts on her instincts and is not afraid to take chances. But she lacks a sense of humanity. When Max's wife asks him about her, he comments, "I'm not sure she's capable of any real feelings. She's the television generation. She learned life from Bugs Bunny. The only reality she knows is what comes over her TV set." And his wife ends their discussion with the warning, "You're in for some dreadful grief, Max." "I know," he confides.

The Group is unusual in that *all* the major characters are women. When *The Group* was released, many critics hailed it as a breakthrough — a real woman's film at last! In fact, however, *The Group* is anything but that. The film follows the eight Vassar girls from the optimism of graduation through their self-discoveries and faded hopes. Helena's opening address to the class becomes ironic. "It is time for the woman to play a role in every sphere of the nation's life," she tells them. In fact, they do nothing of the kind; rather than leaders, they become passive recipients of male domination. They learn nothing and perceive nothing. They seem more interested in the news, gossip and scandal of the group than in the outside world. As Alexander Walker observed, the film represents "womanhood at its rawest and most unflattering."

Marriage seems to become the central concern of "the group." Kay marries a promising playwright. She gives up her own ambitions to help support his, but he drinks and carouses away whatever talent he may have had. He eventually beats, commits and abandons her. Dottie, whose entire adult life is lived in the memory of her brief and humiliating, but somehow magical one-night affair in a seedy Greenwich Village cold-water flat with an embittered artist, marries a wealthy husband with whom, although ostensibly happy, she is really bored beyond endurance. Pokey, about whom we know little, seems to have no other function than to breed prolifically ("Who'da thunk it?"). Priss, the Phi Beta Kappa liberal, marries a pediatrician and, without resistance, allows her marriage to become dictated by his absurd experiments in breast-feeding and toilet-training. Although she boasts of her many affairs and proposals, Libby is actually frigid and terrified of men. Polly, after a brief affair with a well-meaning, but weak-willed, publisher, eventually finds a man who loves her. But Polly must — and seems perfectly willing to — live her life subservient to his.

At the whims of men, the members are variously subjected to seduction, rape, assault, infidelity, impotence, abandonment and domination. The only members of the group who are happy, or seem to be happy, are not associated with men. Helena, who serves the role of observer and chronicler of The Group, stays single and bohemian. Lakey, the most beautiful and mysterious member, also seems to have found satisfaction, but only in a lesbian relationship with a rich and domineering European baroness.

The Group is hardly as cohesive as they would like to be, or seem to be, or pretend to be. Despite the petty bickering and slandering, they somehow feel the need for internal support. As a group, they experiment with sexual mores, political reform, careers, marriages; they confront issues of virginity, frigidity, nursing, contraception, psychoanalysis, neuroticism. Their telephone conversations are endless, Helena's typewriter keeps hammering out personal news items at the bottom of the screen, and they seem to revel in their periodic gatherings, where they exchange the latest gossip and speculation.

Pauline Kael, who observed the making of *The Group*, commented, "As I got to know him, I concluded that, for Lumet, a woman shouldn't have any problems a real man can't take care of. If she does, she's sick." Whether this is Lumet's personal view or not, it certainly seems to be the perception of women in his films.

If women tend not to fare well in Lumet's films, it would follow that marriages don't fare well either. In *The Appointment*, for example, Federico's constant suspicions make life unbearable for his wife. What should have been an ideal marriage becomes a typical Lumet tragedy. Carla prefers suicide to her husband's persecution. A further attack on marriage is exhibited in *Dog Day Afternoon*. Sonny's motivation to rob the bank is to procure the necessary money to finance a sex-change operation for his homosexual wife. (He also has a heterosexual wife, with two children.) The ultimate travesty of marriage occurs in *Last of the Mobile Hot-Shots*. Jeb and Myrtle are married on a TV game show. She wants the kitchen appliances and he wants the money to restore Waverly to its former greatness. Jeb also wants a child to prevent his half-brother, Chicken, from inheriting the delapidated plantation. At the time of their marriage, he doesn't even know her name.

Bad or stale marriages are frequent in Lumet's films: Jabe and Lady in *The*

Fugitive Kind, Eddie and Beatrice in *A View from the Bridge*, James and Mary in *Long Day's Journey into Night*, the various marriages in *The Group*, Dobbs and his wife in *The Deadly Affair*, Federico and Carla in *The Appointment*, Johnson and his wife in *The Offence*, Max and Louise in *Network*, and both Dysart and his wife and Mr. and Mrs. Strang in *Equus*. Val and Lady almost make it in *The Fugitive Kind*. Duke and Ingrid might have made it in *The Anderson Tapes*. Max and Diana never really had a chance in *Network*. But Myrtle and Chicken might make it in *Last of the Mobile Hot-Shots*. Of all Lumet's films, only Red and Kay in *That Kind of Woman* find marital happiness.

LUMET'S CINEMATIC STYLE

Pauline Kael, discussing Lumet's direction, suggests that "Lumet is not so vulgar as most of the new television-trained movie directors who just keep the actors shouting in close-up. And unlike the pretenŝious [sic] ones among them, he knows that he is just shooting a script, that he is not discovering the possibilities in the material and shaping it. . . . From what I observed, Lumet's planning is based on the hope that he'll come out of the shooting with something he can pull together in the editing room." Lumet's version is, expectedly, rather different: "There are no techniques I'm particularly in love with. In fact, quite the reverse. I am rather proud of the fact that I look for *the* technique to tell *that* story. Now I may not always succeed. I'm sure that I have mannerisms that I'm not aware of. I'm sure that I do do certain kinds of camera things, some editing things that are ingrained, that are a part of me. But at least on the conscious level is: *Let's find the technique to tell that story.*"

Rather than consistently favoring one style or technique, Lumet seems inclined to experiment with a diversity of cinematic language. Since Lumet's style is primarily eclectic, what follows is a brief and essentially discursive survey of some of the various techniques he has employed in his films.

Lumet's films are told from an omniscient perspective. His only use of a voice-over omnisicent narrator occurs in *Network*. His only use of the interior monologue occurs in *Lovin' Molly*, in which the three central characters (Gid, Molly and Johnny) narrate their respective sections. His only use of the direct address to the audience, similar to a Greek chorus or a Shakespearian soliloquy, occurs when Dr. Dysart periodically speaks to the audience in *Equus*.

Serpico is Lumet's only film which is nearly all structured as a flashback. The opening scenes show Frank Serpico in an ambulance on his way to the hospital to be treated for a gunshot wound. As the ambulance rushes through the streets of New York, Serpico recalls the events of the past eleven years which have led to the shooting. (*Twelve Angry Men* is interesting, as a contrast, for its total rejection of flashbacks. Instead of revealing the essential narrative information about the crime itself through flashbacks, Lumet chooses to have the proceedings begin and continue without interruption through verbal reconstruction.)

Flashbacks are frequently employed by Lumet as segments to help propel the narrative. For the most part, they are used to communicate important memory sequences which help us to better understand a character's present impasse. These flashback sequences are typically introduced through subliminal editing (also called shock/flash cuts) to reveal the effects of memories that have been repressed into a character's subconscious. They first appear as momentary fragments, disturbing the consciousness. In *The Pawnbroker*, ordinary incidents begin to evoke unwanted and unresolved memories for Nazerman; in *The Offence*, after Johnson has beaten Baxter, momentary glimpses from past cases begin to invade his consciousness. As both films progress, these fragments collect meaning and we are better able to understand the emotional turmoil that is accumulating in the characters' lives.

Flashbacks are typically integrated into the narrative structure as a way of sharing a character's psyche with us. When not being done subliminally, they are usually fully developed narrative sequences. In *Last of the Mobile Hot-Shots*, for example, the flashbacks are used to emphasize Jeb's racist feelings. Although he idealizes his deceased mother, the image retained in his mind is that of his black nanny's nipple. We discover, through flashbacks, that he has created and sustained an image of himself as sexually impotent, helplessly cowering in a corner as his black half-brother enjoys himself with a lovely blonde. This latter image, done in slow motion with expressionistic lighting, particularly preoccupies his thoughts and is repeated several times during the film.

The flashbacks in *Equus* and *Murder on the Orient Express* visualize a character's verbal description of a past event. In *Equus*, as Alan confides to Dysart we frequently see on the screen what he tells. This is often done with Alan's voice-over commentary, as in his first sexual encounter with Nugget in the darkened field, or occasionally using the dialogue of the participants, as in his sexual encounter with Jill Mason. A similar format is employed in *Murder on the Orient Express*. As Poirot interrogates the passengers, they recall incidents from their past; these are typically elaborated upon in flashback views.

Slow motion is used by Lumet in several films, almost always in conjunction with flashback recollections. It is used in the opening pre-credits sequence in *The Pawnbroker*, which is shot silently with a lovely musical score. This slow motion idyll depicts a pleasant family picnic on a pastoral riverside. *The Offence* also opens with a pre-credits slow motion sequence that anticipates the final revelation. In this sequence we see uniformed policemen racing down the corridors to the sounds of a fight (as yet we know nothing more than that). The several flashback diversions in *Last of the Mobile Hot-Shots* are also done in slow motion.

Like Hitchcock (especially in *Rope* and *Lifeboat*), Lumet enjoys the challenge of filming in spatially restricted environments. In *Twelve Angry Men*, we are locked in with the twelve unnamed jurors in their confined room until the long deliberations are finally resolved. In the President's underground chamber in *Fail Safe*, only three items are important: Buck (the translator), the President, and, probably most important, the awesome black telephone that connects the chamber to Moscow. Equally restrictive is Nazerman's cage in *The Pawnbroker*, Dysart's office in *Equus*, the mercantile store in *The Fugitive Kind*, the bank in *Dog Day Afternoon*, the Tyrone drawing room in *Long Day's Journey into Night*, and the train car in *Murder on the Orient Express*. A dramatic example of Lumet's fondness for claustrophobic camera position occurs during a key incident in *The Hill*. When Sergeant Major Wilson faces the rebellious prisoners in the cell block who are protesting the death/murder of Stevens, the camera remains on ground level while following Wilson's towering figure as he bellows to the prisoners. We see his frame, as well as the tiers of shouting prisoners on both sides. The composition of the scene makes the cell block seem as claustrophobic as the jury room, the President's chamber, the pawnshop, the drawing room, the coach.

The "emotional effect" of different lenses become an important factor in Lumet's studied style, especially in *The Hill*. Lumet has repeatedly argued that, primarily as a result of his television training, "one of the first things I do [in planning a film] is literally to lay out a lens plot." In *The Hill*, Lumet used only three lenses. In the first third of the film, *everything* was shot with a 25mm lens; the middle third used a 20mm lens; and the final third used an 18mm lens. The idea for this pattern was to give a sense of increasing constriction and distortion to the film. As opposed to the opening shots, the closing shots are noticeably different in both appearance and effect — especially the close-ups. Using such a lens system, Lumet makes an editorial comment as the film progresses. "That was all part of what we wanted to do," he maintains.

In discussing *Fail Safe* in his book *Science-Fiction Movies*, Philip Strick observes of the underground chamber scenes that "On the hot line was Henry Fonda, filmed Lumet-style in searching close-up against a neutral background and bearing scrutiny with his usual anguished calm." Many observers have mentioned Lumet's proclivity for the close-up, again derived from his television heritage. Lumet himself has defended the close-up: "To me, the close-up is the essence of the cinema." The extreme close-up becomes a dominant visual motif in *Fail Safe*, especially those close-ups of the President meticulously exploring his profile, eyes, lips, ears — all with the care of a biologist studying a specimen under the microscope.

Although not a director to dazzle anyone with his camera pyrotechnics, Lumet is not afraid to move his camera about to create a mood. A much-discussed example of the circular camera appears in *Long Day's Journey into*

Night. When Mary begins to get distraught over Edmund's reminding her of her former "illness" (her narcotics addiction), she begins to chatter nervously and pace around the room. The camera rests in the center of the drawing room and follows her as she anxiously circles the room several times.

Lumet's camera movement often assumes the form of the long take. In *The Fugitive Kind*, before the credits appear, the opening shot has one long take of Val as he explains to the unseen but heard judge the circumstances that led to his attending the "party" and starting the brawl that resulted in his arrest. As he relates the incident, the camera slowly moves around him and gradually in to a close-up. (This single take lasts perhaps five minutes.) In *The Hill*, the long take is again used when the new group of prisoners is escorted on their "excursion" around the hill. Their entire inspection is photographed from atop the hill in a single take following them around the base. The long take is used in *Fail Safe* to build suspense, especially as the President and Buck wait for and engage in the first negotiation with the Russian Premier. The huge black phone appears in close-up in the foreground, Buck on the left and the President on the right; for what often seems an endless period of silence, they wait tensely for the phone to ring.

The long take is used substantially in *Long Day's Journey into Night* and *The Sea Gull*. During Mary's final lament in the former film, the camera slowly and steadily pulls back to a long shot of the family at the table. The gradual pull-back takes nearly two full minutes, before Lumet abruptly cuts to a close-up of Mary. In the latter film, after the parlor game the occupants depart for dinner, leaving Konstantin alone in the room. The camera follows the group as they leave the room (stage right), then the sound track picks up the off-screen voice of Konstantin (who is extreme stage left) reciting his notes for a manuscript he is preparing. Instead of cutting directly to Konstantin, the camera slowly moves across the full length of the room to Konstantin, still reading, and slowly moves closer to him. All this is one continuous take, three minutes in duration, instead of being fragmented by editing from one place to the other.

Lumet also uses the hand-held camera on occasion. It becomes an integral part of *The Pawnbroker*, particularly when Ortiz is racing through the congested streets of Spanish Harlem. It is used to give the film a sense of documentary realism and urgency. The hand-held camera is frequently employed in *The Hill*, especially during the many scenes of punishment as the men make the repeated arduous climb up and down the steep slopes of the hill. Another documentary-like technique is used for a sequence in *The Appointment*. During the interlude in which Carla visits a modeling show at which her former employer oversees the proceedings, the popular *cinéma verité* technique is used to capture the preparations and parades. It is a deliberately unpolished and unsteady sequence.

The aerial shot is utilized for both *The Appointment* and *Bye, Bye Braverman*. When Federico and Carla are making love in the middle of a quiet and remote pasture on the lovely Mediterranean island, the camera steadily pulls up and back to gradually reveal the entire island, the couple eventually becomes a mere microscopic speck. *Bye, Bye Braverman* contains numerous long aerial shots tracking Holly's new red Volkswagen as it meanders along the various streets of Brooklyn (Flatbush, Big Daddy's, Prospect Park), all to a jovial musical accompaniment. Perhaps as much as one-fifth of the film has the characters in the car, photographed in this way.

Although Lumet, like all directors, makes frequent use of parallel editing and cross-cutting, he occasionally uses editing to manipulate time. In *The Anderson Tapes*, during the robbery, three areas of activity are inter-cut: (1) the actual robbery as it progresses, (2) the police outside as they cordon off the street and assault the building, and (3) flash-forward interviews with the victims after the robbery has been thwarted. In *Network*, while the UBS executives are casually discussing the proposed "assassination" of Howard Beale during his program, the visuals inter-cut scenes of the studio audience as they enter and fill the auditorium seats for the show while the vocals continue the discussion without interruption.

Jump cuts are used in *The Appointment*. During Federico's ride on the train back to Rome from Milan, the journey is shown through a series of jump cuts. Later in the same film, jump cuts are used when Carla is idly trying on various pairs of sun glasses. In *Bye, Bye Braverman*, jump cuts are used during Morroe's final fantasy in which he digs his own grave, paints the coffin yellow and buries himself by a driveway outside the cemetery.

The freeze frame is used on two important occasions. At the end of *Fail Safe*, just as "Blackie" has released the nuclear payload over New York City, there are numerous quick scenes of everyday city life. Each of these little fragments, occurring in rapid succession, is terminated with a freeze frame to suggest the very moment that life will end in that particular representative fragment. The freeze frame is also used in *Equus* during Alan's account of his first sexual experience with the horse. As he describes it in a voice-over (to the visual flashback), the frame is frozen at the instant he reaches a sexual climax, then it bleaches to white as he screams.

Lumet is not one for much subjectivity. In *The Hill*, however, there is one incident in which the prisoners are required to wear full field equipment as they trek up and down the hill. On this occasion, so that we share in the agonizing ordeal with one of the prisoners as he wears his stifling gas mask, Lumet frames the camera (hand-held) so that we see with the appropriate masking and hear exaggerated breathing, as he sees and hears.

Lighting contrasts are very important to Lumet. In *The Fugitive Kind*, the lighting pattern abruptly shifts about midway, after Val and Lady have made love for the first time. It suddenly changes from the dingy darkness of the store to the sparkling sunlight as Lady walks down the street. But it returns to darkness shortly afterwards when she discovers that Jabe, her invalid husband, was complicit in her father's murder. In *Equus,* when Alan first goes to the stables, the colors are primarily soft and comfortable browns and golds. Later, after the blinding, when Dysart goes there to question the owner, that richness is gone and it is a cold and empty place. Similar lighting patterns occupy a major function in *Network.* Generally, the film is rather dimly lit. At the stockholder's meeting, for example, when Diana rousingly addresses the guests, they all seem to be featureless bodies concealed in the semi-darkness. Often *Network* seems to be lit from the desk and table lamps that half obscure the faces of the participants. (All this is contrasted to the bright and artificial ceiling lights of the studios and corridors of the UBS building.)

Lumet also employs lighting in an expressionistic style. The memory sequences in *Last of the Mobile Hot-Shots, The Offence* and *Equus* all have an unrealistic, but highly expressive, aura to them. To dramatize both Jeb's nostalgia for Waverly and his impotence with the prostitute, Lumet uses expressionistic lighting effects. When Jeb, for example, wheels his chair on to the balcony, a red glow covers the area; it is soft and quiet as he affectionately remembers the past greatness and fantasizes about the future. The yellow-orange glow which covers the memory fragments of Sergeant Johnson in *The Offence* as he visualizes the assaulted child seem idyllic and romantic. When Alan is in the loft above the stable with Jill, the lighting changes in *Equus* from the normal to a lush yellow, as Alan recalls his unresolved sexual conflict.

The lighting in *Child's Play* is highly complex. It begins in daylight with bright colors. As the strange events increase in frequency and violence, the lighting gradually becomes darker and more sinister. Especially important to the film are the scenes in the chapel — lit mainly from the reddish glow of the burning candles. As the film opens, the peaceful reddish glow covers the chapel. About midway in the film, the two rival teachers accidentally meet in the chapel. When Malley enters he is unaware that Dobbs is present, half-hidden in the darkness at the back. Dobbs tells Malley of an anecdote about the candle. "I remember in grade school, years ago, the sisters telling us that God himself was present on the altar whenever that little red light was burning. I used to think, 'What if a wind should blow into the church and find that light?' Pffff. No more God." And, predictably, the candle is extinguished twice: once when the statue of Christ is replaced by a boy in a mock crucifixion, and again at the end when Dobbs is ominously surrounded by the boys. In some way, the light does indicate the presence of good (when all is calm) and evil (when violence occurs).

In a number of films, Lumet uses no music. There is no musical accompaniment in *Long Day's Journey into Night, Fail Safe* or *The Hill.* As opposed to the lush orchestral music that fills the background of *Murder on the Orient Express*, which is a deliberate throwback to the thirties, music is generally used very sparingly by Lumet. In *Serpico*, for example, the music is sentimental and only used during tender moments, of which there are comparatively few. Especially at times of crisis in *Serpico*, which seem to be many, Lumet rejects any musical backgrounds, preferring the use of natural sounds.

Musical themes often play an important function in Lumet's films. In *Child's Play*, for example, music occurs only at moments of unnatural events (a beating, a threat, a confrontation). Generally, it is used only at critical times. Rather than melodic, the music is similar to a liturgical chant, foreboding and sinister, or a variation on a boys' choral song. With only one exception, there is a total absence of peaceful music; that exception occurs when Dobbs speaks of his affection for "the boys" after Reis has lacerated himself and confessed his fear of the school.

In *The Group*, theme music becomes a dominant leitmotif. The school choral song is heard during the opening credits' montage of the girls; they are filled with youthful energy and enthusiasm. This idealism becomes ironic, since the theme music then is used when the girls experience a disruption, rejection, failure or defeat. It is heard when Lakey leaves for Europe, when Dottie is humiliated in Washington Square Park, when Priss marries Sloan, when Helena is told that Kay had called her a "neuter," when Priss loses her job, when Libby, a virgin, is rejected by Nils, when Sloan censures Priss for succumbing to bottle feeding, when Gus leaves Polly, when Harald leaves Kay after her release from the hospital, when the radio announces Hitler's aggression in Europe, and at the ending (which repeats the opening valedictory address in a voice-over) on the way to the cemetery.

For the most part, mechanical sounds replace music in Lumet's films. Although there is no background music in *The Hill*, there is almost constant background noise. When in the punishment area, for example, in the background are heard the drill commands and responses which are always loud, rapid, irritating and formal. The sounds of electronic surveillance devices are heard throughout *The Anderson Tapes*: buzzers, alarms, bleeps, scramblers, rewinds. There is also no music in *Fail Safe*. Most sounds are from mechanical equipment: microphones, feedback, tapes, pulses, telephones, various signals and computer sounds. The computer machinery is ever-present in the background of the Omaha base, just as the engine noise is ever-present in the cockpit of the bomber. All this is contrasted to the lengthy periods of utter anticipatory silence that accompany the President in the underground shelter.

CONCLUSION

Graham Petrie concludes his article on "The Films of Sidney Lumet" with a general consideration of Lumet's stature: "Fortunately Lumet has been in an extremely enviable position from the very beginning of his career: from *Twelve Angry Men* onwards, he has made only those films which he has wanted to make, and he has made them in conditions of almost complete independence. . . . Although he does not write his own scripts, it is clear from statements he has made in interviews, and from the finished products, that the ultimate decision on what is to be filmed and how it is to be filmed is his own."

Although Petrie's insightful but cursory study was made a decade ago, his conclusion remains valid. Lumet has enjoyed both considerable independence and artistic control. He has suggested in an interview with the author, "Only one person can say 'print.' And only one vision can really emerge in a work." Lumet assumes responsibility for his films, both the successes and the failures.

Certainly, at present, Sidney Lumet is, critically, an underrated director. Perhaps it is because his career has had such a dramatic diversity of smashes and flops that he is often regarded less for his personal contributions than for his technical skills. If this brief survey of Lumet's films supports any common thesis, that thesis, I believe, has been best expressed by Lumet himself: "I can't say I have a *philosophy* of directing. I have a feeling of wanting to be moved by what I am working on. Wanting to be deeply emotionally involved, wanting it to mean something *to me.*"

NOTES

1. Maurice Yacowar. *Tennessee Williams and Film* (New York: Ungar, 1977).
2. Anon. *Playboy*, (22 October 1975).
3. Alexander Walker. *London Evening Standard* (18 December 1975).
4. John Simon. *Esquire* (March 1974).
5. *See also* Lumet's "Why Am I Happy?," *Newsweek*, 57 (12 June 1961).

The Films: Synopses, Credits and Notes

1 TWELVE ANGRY MEN (1957)

Outside of a brief prologue and epilogue, the entire film takes place using only a single set, the jury room. The twelve jury members have been instructed by the judge to render their verdict on the eighteen year old boy accused of patricide; either guilty if there is sufficient cause (which would carry a death sentence) or not guilty if there is a reasonable doubt (which the judge stresses).

After this brief prologue, as the credits appear on the screen, the jurors file into the jury room and congregate around the long table to talk. The jurors are referred to and called by their numbers only. There seems to be little doubt that the slum boy is guilty, but when the vote is taken one jury member dissents. Juror Number Eight (Fonda) is not convinced the boy is innocent, but he believes there is a reasonable cause for discussion. "I don't know," he tells the others. "I just want to talk. . . . It's not easy to raise my hand and send a boy off to his death without talking about it." It is a hot day, and the other members are impatient and reluctant, but Number Eight insists on reviewing the evidence.

They begin to discuss the murder weapon. The knife found in the body was assumed to be the boy's seemingly unusual one. Number Eight takes out an identical knife and claims he bought it at a nearby pawn shop. This establishes "reasonable doubt" for some, and when the second vote is taken Number Two (Fielder) changes his vote to not guilty, saying he wants to hear more.

As the heat of the day wears on and the tension among the jurors intensifies, we gradually get to know each member's personality and characteristics. Number Seven (Warden) has tickets for a baseball game that night and wants to get his inconvenient duty over with quickly. Number Twelve (Webber) is an advertising executive but highly indecisive about the case. He keeps changing his vote from guilty to not guilty to guilty. Number Four (Marshall) is a stock broker, always emotionally composed and neatly groomed (one juror comments that he "never sweats"), who is evidentially convinced of the boy's guilt. The most orderly of the jury, he presents his arguments with eloquence. Number Ten (Begley), who grew up in the slums himself, now owns three garages. Since he worked himself out of the slums, he harbors powerful resentments against all slum-kids.

Other aspects of the case are questioned: Why would the boy return to the scene of the crime three hours later? Why would he leave the knife in the body? How could the downward angle of the knife be explained? The figurative use of the threat "I'm going to kill you" and the credibility of the two witnesses are also discussed. By the fifth vote, nine of the jury members have voted not guilty. Disinterested and anxious to leave, Number Seven goes along with the others. Number Four is finally convinced that a "reasonable doubt" does exist. Number Three (Cobb) sees himself as the boy's personal executioner as a symbolic act against his own rebellious son and is the last to change his vote to not guilty.

The last shot is a slow dissolve of the jury table over the court house. The jury members file singly out of the room.

Credits

Producers:	Henry Fonda and Reginald Rose
Director:	Sidney Lumet
Story and Screenplay:	Reginald Rose, from his original teleplay
Director of Photography:	Boris Kaufman
Art Direction:	Robert Markell
Music:	Kenyon Hopkins
Sound:	James Gleason
Editor:	Carl Lerner
Associate Producer:	George Justin
Cast:	Henry Fonda (Juror No. 8, "Davis"), Lee J. Cobb (Juror No. 3), Ed Begley (Juror No. 10), E. G. Marshall (Juror No. 4), Jack Warden (Juror No. 7), Martin Balsam (Juror No. 1), John Fielder (Juror No. 2), Jack Klugman (Juror No. 5), Edward Binns (Juror No. 6), Joseph Sweeney (Juror No. 9), George Voskovec (Juror No. 11), Robert Webber (Juror No. 12), Rudy Bond (Judge), James A. Kelly (Guard), Bill Nelson (Court Clerk), John Savoca (Defendant).
Filmed in New York	
Distribution:	United Artists
Running Time:	95 minutes
Release:	April, 1957

Note

Although the film won no Academy Awards, it collected three nominations: best picture, best director, and best screenplay based upon material from another medium. The Directors Guild of America gave its best director award to Lumet. Henry Fonda won the British Film Academy prize for best actor. The film itself won the Golden Bear (first prize) award at the Berlin Festival.

2 STAGE STRUCK (1958)

Eva Lovelace (Strasberg), born as Gertrude Lengenfelder, has done summer work in her small Vermont hometown. Although very young and inexperienced, she comes to New York filled with confidence and determination to be a star on Broadway. Through a meeting with the established actor Robert Hedges (Marshall), who assumes a fatherly interest in her career, she gets a brief introduction to an influential producer, Lewis Easton (Fonda), and a young playwright, Joe Sheridan (Plummer). She is given an audition but so overacts a one-line part that Easton shrugs her off.

Sheridan later meets Eva by chance and takes her to the opening night party of his play at Easton's penthouse residence. While at the party, Eva asks Sheridan, "Don't you think one can obtain anything?" to which Sheridan replies, "I think a person can aim high and land in the gutter." Eva, unused to champagne and celebrities, quickly becomes inebriated. Carried away by her love for the theatre, she begins to recite the balcony scene from *Romeo and Juliet*. Unaware of the intimacy of her feelings, the guests amuse themselves at her expense. But Hedges, more sensitive to what the moment means to her, recites Romeo's lines. Both Easton and Sheridan are impressed. She stays the night with Easton, but the next morning he regrets his action. Easton meets with Sheridan later that morning in the park to discuss his dilemma over Eva. He asks Sheridan to act as an intermediary to inform Eva that he does not share her love and wants the affair to end. Sheridan is upset but, with sensitivity, reluctantly tells Eva.

Heartbroken and defeated, Eva vainly persists to find work in the theatre. Sheridan eventually finds Eva reciting the poetry of Poe and Housman in a Greenwich Village bistro. He is so inspired by her reading and feeling that he secretly rehearses her for the lead in his new play, since he is unhappy with Easton's choice of Rita Vernon (Greenwood), an established star. The day before opening night, Rita decides the part is not suited for her and demands that Sheridan rewrite it. Upon his refusal, she threatens to have "pneumonia." Easton, who now knows Eva is prepared to go on, gives her the chance. She proves to be a brilliant success on her first night. Both Easton and Sheridan propose marriage but Eva refuses, realizing that her career in the theatre must come before everything else.

Credits

Producer:	Stuart Millar
Director:	Sidney Lumet
Screenplay:	Ruth and Augustus Goetz, based on the play "Morning Glory" by Zoe Akins
Directors of Photography:	Franz F. Planer and Maurice Hartzband
Art Direction:	Kim Edgar Swandos
Music:	Alex North
Sound:	James A. Gleason, Terry Kellum

Costume Designer:	Moss Mabry
Editor:	Stuart Gilmore
Production Supervisor:	George Justin
Production Assistant:	Stephen Bono
Assistant Director:	Charles H. Maguire
Second Assistant Director:	William C. Garrity
In Charge of Production:	William Dozier
Make-up:	Bob Jiras
Hairdresser:	Willis Hanchett
Cast:	Henry Fonda (Lewis Easton), Susan Strasberg (Eva Lovelace), Joan Greenwood (Rita Vernon), Herbert Marshall (Robert Hedges), Christopher Plummer (Joe Sheridan), Daniel Ocko (Constantine), Pat Harrington (Benny), Frank Campanella (Victor), John Fielder (Adrian), Patricia Englund (Gwen Hall), Jack Weston (Frank), Sally Gracie (Elizabeth), Nina Hansen (Regina), Harold Grau (Stage Doorman)
Filmed on location in New York	
Distribution:	RKO-Radio (Buena Vista)
Running Time:	95 minutes
Color:	Technicolor
Release:	March, 1958

3 THAT KIND OF WOMAN (1959)

The year is 1944 and the place is a train from Miami to New York. Kay (Loren), a beautiful brunette, and her companion, Jane (Nichols), are aboard. Harry Corwin (Wynn), under the orders of his millionaire employer, accompanies the two women. The millionaire, referred to as "The Man" (Sanders), gets war-time contracts by influencing generals and admirals with his lovely mistresses — Kay is one of them. The train is filled with servicemen. Kay meets Red (Hunter), a twenty-three year old paratrooper, in the club car. Red is on his last leave home before going overseas. Red's friend, Kelly (Warden), is also there. Kay teases Red, saying that he does not even look old enough to drink, but Red tells her that he is old enough to do "anything." Kay enjoys the company of the soldiers and ends up spending the night with Red.

Kay leaves Red at the station, but Red and Kelly are able to find the millionaire's mansion and follow the two women there. "The Man" is one of the wealthiest and most powerful magnates in the country. He and Kay get along well, and he takes very good care of her. But Red is persistent in his pursuit of her. When the millionaire realizes Red is in love with Kay, and she with him, he proposes to her. He gives Kay time to think. Meanwhile, Red perseveres and courts her in Central Park, Staten Island and Grand Central Station. Kay must decide between the luxury and comfort the millionaire could provide and the love she could enjoy with Red. At the last minute, before Red is to leave, Kay rushes to the railway station to go to Vermont with him to meet his family.

Credits

Producer:	Carlo Ponti, Marcello Girosi
Director:	Sidney Lumet
Screenplay:	Walter Bernstein, from a story by Robert Lowry
Photography:	Boris Kaufman
Art Direction:	Hal Pereira, Roland Anderson
Music:	Daniele Amfitheatrof
Sound:	James Gleason, Charles Grenzbach
Editor:	Howard Smith
Associate Producer:	Ray Wander
Cast:	Sophia Loren (Kay), Tab Hunter (Red), George Sanders (The Man), Jack Warden (Kelly), Barbara Nichols (Jane), Keenan Wynn (Harry).
Filmed in New York	
Distribution:	Paramount
Running Time:	92 minutes
Release:	September, 1959

4 THE FUGITIVE KIND (1960)

Valentine Xavier (Brando) is a thirty year old drifter who has been earning his living as a night-club guitarist. He is identified with his snakeskin jacket and his guitar, which he calls his "life's companion." Val is asked to play at a party in New Orleans and, although he does not want to, he goes. Someone at the party laughs at his playing and he starts a fight. (There were also illicit activities going on at the party.) After fighting, Val is arrested.

As the film opens, Val recounts the circumstances of his arrest to a New Orleans judge, relating how his life sickens him and how he wants to change. He tells the judge, "You're not young at thirty when you've been on a party since you were sixteen." Val promises not to return to New Orleans and, resolved to change his ways, arrives one stormy night in the town of Two Fingers, Mississippi. The men in town are hunting an escaped convict. Val is befriended by a kindly and understanding woman named Vee Talbot (Stapleton), the wife of the sheriff (Armstrong). She offers to let him stay the night in the detention cell from which the convict had escaped. She also helps him get a job as a clerk at the Torrance Mercantile Store. Dying of cancer, Jabe Torrance (Jory), the owner of the store, is brought from the hospital back to Two Fingers and promptly confined to his bed on the second floor of the store. Since Jabe is bed-ridden, his wife, Lady (Magnani), manages the store. Lady is the daughter of an Italian winegrower who had lived outside of town. She is haunted by memories of the night vigilantes killed her father by setting fire to his garden because he had sold liquor to blacks.

A gradual attraction develops between Val and Lady, but this is complicated by the frequent visits of Carol Cutrere (Woodward). Carol, a free-spirited nymph, is the outcast daughter of the wealthiest family in the county, who pay her to live in the next county. She shows her attraction for Val in a cemetery but he declines.

When Val sees trouble starting with his relationship with Lady, he decides to leave town. Unable to break the bond with Lady, which has given his life a new meaning, he returns and helps her build a confectionery at the rear of the mercantile. Jabe, still vicious toward Lady and still confined to his bed, is suspicious of the relationship between Lady and Val, especially when he is informed that Lady has taken Val to see the burned garden of her father. Jabe's meddlesome nurse (Chew) tells him that Lady is pregnant with Val's child. In the heat of a consequent argument with Lady, Jabe angrily tells her that he had been a part of the vigilante gang that killed her father. Embittered by Lady's determination to finish the confectionery, Jabe sets it on fire. Outraged, Lady tries to stop him but Jabe shoots her before she can do anything. Val, rushing to Lady's defense, is pushed back into the blaze by the force from a fire hose held by the sheriff and some hostile townspeople.

Later, as Carol wanders through the ruins, she finds Val's snakeskin jacket and remarks, "Wild things leave skins behind them."

Credits

Producers:	Martin Jurow and Richard A. Shepherd
Director:	Sidney Lumet
Screenplay:	Tennessee Williams and Meade Roberts, based on Williams' play *Orpheus Descending*
Photography:	Boris Kaufman
Art Direction:	Richard Sylbert
Set Decoration:	Gene Challahan
Music Composed and Conducted by:	Kenyon Hopkins
Sound:	James Gleason and Philip Gleason
Costumes:	Frank Thompson
Editor:	Carl Lerner
Assistant Director:	Charles H. Maguire
Associate Producer:	George Justin
Cast:	Marlon Brando (Val Xavier), Anna Magnani (Lady Torrance), Joanne Woodward (Carol Cutrere), Maureen Stapleton (Vee Talbot), Victor Jory (Jabe Torrance), R. G. Armstrong (Sheriff Talbot), Emory Richardson (Uncle Pleasant, the Conjure Man), Spivy (Ruby Lightfoot),

Sally Gracie (Dolly Hamma), Lucille Benson (Beulah Binnings), John Baragrey (David Cutrere), Ben Yaffee (Dog Hamma), Joe Brown, Jr. (Pee Wee Binnings), Virgilia Chew (Nurse Porter), Frank Borgman (Gas Station Attendant), Janice Mars (Attendant's Wife), Debbie Lynch (Lonely Girl).

Filmed in New York and on location in Milton, New York
Distribution: United Artists
Running time: 119, 135 minutes
Release: May, 1960

Note

Joanne Woodward won the Sebastian Festival prize for Best Female Interpretation.

5 A VIEW FROM THE BRIDGE (1961)

Eddie Carbone (Vallone) is a tough and robust Italian-American longshoreman who works on the Brooklyn waterfront. He and his wife, Beatrice (Stapleton), have raised her niece, Catherine (Lawrence), from infancy, when she was orphaned.

Catherine is now eighteen and the joy of Eddie's otherwise drab life. Beatrice is somewhat neglected by Eddie because of his devotion to Catherine but nevertheless remains faithful to him and the family. Eddie seems to have more than a fatherly affection for Catherine but refuses to acknowledge it. Two of Beatrice's cousins, Marco (Pellegrin) and Rodolpho (Sorel), enter the United States illegally and stay at the Carbone house. Marco has a wife and two children; Rodolpho is twenty-two and very attractive. Eddie finds them both jobs and keeps secret the fact that they are illegal immigrants. An attraction grows between Rodolpho and Catherine, which Eddie cannot accept; Eddie thinks Rodolpho wants to marry Catherine to gain U.S. citizenship. Eddie becomes antagonistic toward Rodolpho, suggesting that he is distinctly feminine. When this does not change Catherine's feelings, Eddie openly accuses Rodolpho of being a homosexual and attempts to degrade him by kissing him on the lips. This action only further estranges Catherine from Eddie, and she and Rodolpho announce their plan to marry. Beatrice is upset by Eddie's obsession and encourages Catherine to run away with Rodolpho. In desperation, Eddie consults Alfieri (Carnovsky), a local lawyer. Alfieri tells Eddie there is nothing wrong with Catherine and Rodolpho's relationship. This fills Eddie with so much rage that he goes to the immigration authorities to report Marco and Rodolpho.

On the eve of Rodolpho's wedding to Catherine, the authorities apprehend Marco and Rodolpho. Marco spits on Eddie and denounces him in front of his neighbors. Alfieri bails them out and arranges Rodolpho's freedom because of his plans to marry Catherine; but Marco is scheduled to be deported. He goes to Eddie's house and challenges him to a fight. After a brutal street fight, Marco forces Eddie to his knees. Humiliated, frustrated and disgraced, Eddie plunges a dock-worker's hook into his heart.

Credits

Producer:	Paul Graetz
Director:	Sidney Lumet
Screenplay:	Norman Rosten, based on Arthur Miller's play
Photography:	Michel Kelber
Art Direction:	Jacques Saulnier
Music:	Maurice Leroux
Sound:	Jo deBretagne
Editor:	Francoise Javet
Assistant Director:	Dossia Mage
Production Manager:	Julien Riviere
Cast:	Raf Vallone (Eddie Carbone), Jean Sorel (Rodolpho), Maureen Stapleton (Beatrice Carbone), Carol Lawrence (Catherine), Raymond Pellegrin (Marco), Morris Carnovsky (Mr. Alfieri), Harvey Lembeck (Mike), Mickey Knox (Louis), Vincent Gardenia (Lipari), Frank Campanella (Longshoreman).
Filmed in Paris and on location in Brooklyn, New York	
Distribution:	Paramount
Running Time:	114 minutes
Release:	1961
European title:	*Vu Du Pont*

Note

The film was released in both a French and an English version.

6 LONG DAY'S JOURNEY INTO NIGHT (1962)

This film recounts a single, important day in the lives of the Tyrone family. The film begins with the family enjoying the morning sunshine on the porch of their New London, Connecticut summer home. It is a pleasant day in 1912; the house is in need of repair. James Tyrone (Richardson) is a self-righteous, aging theatrical performer with a dread of ending up in "the poor house." James' wife, Mary (Hepburn), has just returned from a sanatorium, presumably cured of her addiction to morphine. Their oldest son, Jamie (Robards), has tried to follow in his father's footsteps as an actor, but his attempts have been only half-hearted, which has turned him into a cynic who only finds relief in alcohol. The younger son, Edmund (Stockwell), a writer, is twenty-three. He spent several years at sea but has returned because he fears he has consumption.

Nearly all the film takes place after the family moves indoors to the parlor, where James says there is a "gloom in the air that you can cut with a knife." The afternoon is hot and at sunset fog begins to roll in from the sea. It is evident as the evening proceeds that Mary is not, in fact, cured. She is very worried about Edmund's condition and although she will not consciously face it, she fears it is consumption. Rather than confront it directly, she periodically retreats to her room, where she resumes her addiction. The rest of the family also fear the worst about Edmund's condition but nervously wait for the doctor to call. The family has a series of harsh arguments where long-suppressed jealousies and resentments are finally released. James tries to explain his miserliness as Jamie gets drunk, and tells Edmund that at the same time he both loves and hates him. Mary is mentally and physically moving away from the family and in her euphoric condition recalls the events of her life, especially her early years with James. The doctor phones to confirm that Edmund does, indeed, have consumption. James has planned to send Edmund to a cheap state institution for treatment, but Jamie insists that they place Edmund in a private sanatorium where he will receive better care.

As night descends, the family seems temporarily reconciled.

Credits

Producer:	Ely Landau
Director:	Sidney Lumet
Screenplay:	Eugene O'Neill's play
Photography:	Boris Kaufman
Art Direction:	Richard Sylbert
Music Composed and Played by:	Andre Previn
Costumes:	Motley
Production Supervisor:	George Justin
Editor:	Ralph Rosenblum
Cast:	Katherine Hepburn (Mary Tyrone), Ralph Richardson (James Tyrone Sr.), Jason Robards, Jr. (Jamie Tyrone), Dean Stockwell (Edmund Tyrone), Jeanne Barr (Kathleen the Maid).
Filmed in New York	
Distribution:	20th Century-Fox
Running Time:	originally 174, cut to 136 minutes
Release:	1962

Note

At the Cannes Film Festival, all four actors (Hepburn, Richardson, Robards and

Stockwell) won the prize for best acting *ex-aequo* with *A Taste of Honey*. Katherine Hepburn was nominated for an Academy Award, and Lumet again won the Directors Guild award for best director.

7 FAIL SAFE (1964)

The opening of the film establishes four areas of activity. It begins with General Black (O'Herlihy) in New York, whose prophetic dream about a bullfight is interrupted by the alarm clock; while at a party in Washington D.C., Professor Groeteschele (Matthau), a political scientist, amuses the guests with projections about thermo-nuclear war; also at the same time at the strategic Air Command Base in Omaha, preparations are being made to show visiting officials the safeguard facilities; and in Anchorage, Alaska, Colonel Grady (Binns) readies his bomber crew for a routine mission.

While General Bogan (Overton) and Colonel Cascio (Weaver) are demonstrating the safeguards of the fail-safe mechanism which controls America's nuclear operations to Congressman Raskob (Booke) and Mr. Knapp (Collins), an unidentified object is noticed and the system goes into a routine alert. The planes are directed to converge on their Soviet targets. At the Pentagon, Professor Groeteschele is lecturing the Joint Chiefs on the inadvisability of limited war, while General Black argues the absurdity of modern pushbutton warfare. When the unidentified object is discovered to be an off-course commercial flight, the bombers are recalled. A malfunction in the fault indicator, however, sends one bomber group, Group Six, under Grady's command, heading toward its target: Moscow. Knapp, whose company built many of the safety devices, mentions the growing "likelihood of *subtle* errors that can occur." General Black comments at this point, "Something failed — a man, a machine — it doesn't matter — it was bound to happen sooner or later." The Russians have jammed the radio equipment of Group Six so that Grady cannot be contacted in time to be recalled. Once he has crossed the fail-safe point, he has been instructed to stay on course and, as trained, will not respond to vocal orders.

The President, stationed in his subterranean bunker, deciding what the best course of action would be, speaks to his advisors around the country. Professor Groeteschele, functioning as a civilian advisor, feels the United States should utilize this opportunity to defeat the Soviet Union by surprise ("History demands it"). General Black, on the other hand, recommends caution and recommends that the United States should do anything to prevent nuclear warfare. The President orders the planes in Group Six to be shot down. With the help of his interpreter, Buck (Hagman), the President tries to convince the Soviet Premier, who knows of the approaching bombers, that this is not an intentional sneak attack. The attempt to shoot down the planes fails and the President orders General Bogan to have Colonel Cascio give any information, no matter how secret, to the Russians to help prevent the bombers from reaching Moscow. Under the strain of collaborating with the Russians, Colonel Cascio has a mental breakdown and has to be restrained. The Russians lift the radio jamming, but despite orders from the

President and pleas from his wife, Colonel Grady continues as his training has prescribed. While talking to the Russian Premier about the eventuality of one of the bombers reaching the target, the President regretfully says, "We're to blame — both of us — we let our machines get out of hand. . . . We're responsible for what happens to us. . . . Today we had a taste of the future — what do we say to the dead?"

Colonel Grady maneuvers through the Russian defenses to drop his bombs on Moscow. To prevent escalating retaliation, the President orders an equal payload of bombs dropped on New York City. General Black empties his bombs on New York City and then poisons himself.

Credits

Producer:	Max E. Youngstein
Director:	Sidney Lumet
Screenplay:	Walter Bernstein, based on the novel by Eugene Burdick and Harvey Wheeler
Director of Photography:	Gerald Hirschfeld
Art Direction:	Albert Brenner
Set Decoration:	J. C. Delaney
Sound:	Jack Fitzstephens, William Swift
Costumes:	Anna Hill Johnstone
Editor:	Ralph Rosenblum
Sound Editor:	Jack Fitzstephens
Sound Mixer:	William Swift
Assistant Director:	Harry Falk, Jr.
Associate Producer:	Charles H. Maquire
Special and Animated Effects:	Storyboard, Inc.
Camera Operator:	Al Taffett
Chief Electrician:	Howard Fortune
Chief Grip:	Edward Knott
Continuity:	Marguerite James
Make-up:	Harry Buchman
Titles:	F. Hillsberg, Inc.
Cast:	Henry Fonda (The President), Dan O'Herlihy (General Black), Walter Matthau (Groeteschele), Frank Overton (General Bogan), Edward Binns (Colonel Grady), Fritz Weaver (Colonel Cascio), Larry Hagman (Buck), William Hansen (Secretary Swenson), Rullel Hardie (General Stark), Russell Collins (Knapp), Sorrell Booke (Congressman Raskob), Nancy Berg (Ilsa Wolfe), John Connell (Thomas), Frank Simpson (Sullivan), Hildy Parks (Betty Black), Janet Ward (Mrs. Grady), Dom DeLouise (Sgt. Collins), Dana Elcar (Foster), Stuart Germain (Mr. Cascio), Louise Larabee (Mrs. Cascio), Frieda Altman (Jennie), Bob Gerringer (Fly).

74 / SIDNEY LUMET

Filmed in
  New York
Distribution: BLC/Columbia
Running Time: 112 minutes
Release: October, 1964

8   THE PAWNBROKER (1965)

Sol Nazerman (Steiger) had been a professor in Germany before World War II. Because he is Jewish, he and his family were imprisoned in a Nazi concentration camp. He is now haunted by guilt because only he, of his family, survived the ordeal of the camp. Now, hardened and unfeeling, he is a pawnbroker in New York's Spanish Harlem.

The date is September 29, and the personal significance of this particular date begins to release memories that he has suppressed for nearly two decades. Jesus Ortiz (Sanchez), an ambitious young Puerto Rican, works as an apprentice under Nazerman, insistently wanting to learn to become a pawnbroker himself. Ortiz wants to be closer to Nazerman but is continually distanced by Nazerman's paralytic insensitivity. Marilyn Birchfield (Fitzgerald), a neighborhood social worker, tries to persuade Nazerman to contribute money and time in an effort to help the young people of Harlem, but she is also rejected by him. Nazerman has completely isolated himself from the world, treating everyone as "scum."

Despite his deliberate suppression of the events at Auschwitz, casual incidents that occur during this day evoke unwanted memories: a street fight reminds him of an attempted escape in the camp, the social worker reminds him of his dead wife, a young girl who wants to pawn an engagement ring reminds him of the Nazi confiscation of jewelry. The backer of the pawnshop, Rodriquez (Peters), a black underworld figure who has become wealthy by exploiting the poor and helpless, uses the shop to cover up illegal activities. Nazerman has prospered because of this but has also refused to acknowledge the source of his supplemental income.

While teaching Ortiz about "gold," Ortiz admiringly asks Nazerman, "How do *you people* come to business so easily?" Nazerman, aroused to anger over the phrase "you people," instills in Ortiz his belief that "next to the speed of light, which Einstein says is the only absolute, next to that and only that, *I rate money.*" Ortiz mistakes Nazerman's bitter dictum as a universal justification to procure money by any means. Ortiz reveals his obsession for money to set up his own shop to his girlfriend (Oliver), a prostitute working for Rodriquez. Worried that Ortiz will resort to something illegal and dangerous, the well-meaning woman offers herself to Nazerman in a "private session" for extra money. She casually discloses the network of prostitution that supports Rodriquez. This horrible revelation awakens in Nazerman the unbearable realization for the first time that the money which keeps him and his dependents in affluence is derived from the same kind of human suffering that he witnessed in Auschwitz. When he confronts Rodriquez with this, Rodriquez makes him admit (by default) to complicity. Nazerman, in emotional agony, begs to be let out of the business, but Rodriquez will not allow it.

Ortiz's former friends make fun of him for working so hard (and honestly) in a pawnshop, but he tells them of all the money he has seen Nazerman put in the safe. Nazerman, finally and fully shocked into the reality of his complicity, spends the night aimlessly wandering the neon streets of New York. The following morning, he goes to Miss Birchfield's apartment where he verbalizes his internal crisis to her. Returning to the pawnshop, he assumes an irrational perspective, giving excessive amounts of money to customers for worthless items and practically nothing for valuable items. He also refuses to sign certain financially important papers for Rodriquez, even though he knows (and hopes) that it puts his life in jeopardy. Ortiz again tries to win some reassurance from Nazerman, only to again be rejected. Ortiz then goes to his friends and arranges for them to rob the pawnshop. When Ortiz and the hoodlums arrive, Nazerman refuses to give them the money and goads them into shooting. Ortiz, at the last moment, prevents Nazerman from being shot but is himself fatally wounded. Ortiz dies in Nazerman's arms. Nazerman, horrified, pushes his palm through a paper spindle as a physical expression of his internal pain.

Credits

Producers:	Roger H. Lewis and Philip Langner
Director:	Sidney Lumet
Screenplay:	David Friedkin and Morton Fine, based on the novel by Edward Lewis Wallant
Photography:	Boris Kaufman
Art Direction:	Richard Sylbert
Set Decoration:	Jack Flaherty
Music:	Quincy Jones
Sound:	Dennis Maitland
Costumes:	Anna Hill Johnstone
Editor:	Ralph Rosenblum
Associate Producer:	Joseph Manduke
Executive Producer:	Worthington Miner
Production Manager:	Ulu Grosbard
Assistant Director:	Dan Eriksen
Make-up:	Bill Herman
Production Head:	Alfred Markim
Cast:	Rod Steiger (Sol Nazerman), Geraldine Fitzgerald (Marilyn Birchfield), Brock Peters (Rodriquez), Jaime Sanchez (Jesus Ortiz), Thelma Oliver (Ortiz' Girl), Marketa Kimbrell (Tessie), Baruch Lumet (Mendel), Juano Hernandez (Mr. Smith, the Philosopher), Linda Geiser (Ruth), Nancy R. Pollock (Bertha), Raymond St. Jacques (Tangee), John McCurry (Buck), Charles Dierkop (Robin-

son), Eusebia Cosme (Mrs. Ortiz), Warren Finnerty (Savarese), Jack Ader (Morton), Marianne Kanter (Joan), E. M. Margolese (Papa).

Filmed in
  New York
Distribution: Planet-Landau/Allied Artists
Running Time: 115 minutes
Release: April, 1965

Note

Rod Steiger won both the British Film Academy and Berlin Film Festival awards for best actor and was nominated for an Academy Award.

9 THE HILL (1965)

During World War II, five new prisoners arrive at a desert stockade in North Africa which is being used as a British Military detention camp. In the middle of the fort rises a towering thirty-five foot man-made hill of sand and rock which is used for punishment — the prisoners are made to run up and down the hill carrying full packs. The prisoners are: Jock McGrath (Watson), who attacked three members of the Military Police; George Stevens (Lynch), who in an attempt to visit his wife in England went AWOL; Jacko King (Davis), a Jamaican who stole liquor from the Sergeant's Mess; Monty Bartlett (Kinnear), a Cockney who had nine previous army sentences before stealing motor tires; and Warrant Officer Joe Roberts (Connery), who was court-martialled for cowardice. (It is later revealed that Roberts had refused an insane order that would have resulted in certain death.)

These five prisoners are put in the same cell under the discipline of a new officer at the prison, Staff Sergeant Williams (Hendry). Because of the incompetence of the stockade Commandant (Bird), who prefers to spend his time in town with local whores than at the camp with prison affairs, punishment procedures are administered under the direction of Regimental Sergeant Major Wilson (Andrews). Wilson is dedicated to the belief that harsh discipline will turn the wayward prisoners back into good soldiers. Williams makes it his personal vendetta to "break" Roberts, because he was a respected officer, and Jacko King, because he is black; he tells Roberts, "The court-martial busted you, but I'm going to finish the job."

The prisoners are given a very superficial physical examination by the disillusioned and disinterested camp Medical Officer (Redgrave). Roberts observes to a companion, "We're all doing time, even the screws." Stevens is very weak and cannot make the excessive strenuous climbs. Staff Harris (Bannen), who seems genuinely concerned over the prisoners, advises Wilson about Williams' excessive punishment, but Wilson refuses to intervene. Under the stress of Williams' constant harassment, Stevens has a mental breakdown and dies. The other prisoners, incensed by the useless death of Stevens, accuse the sadistic Williams of the murder of their fellow inmate. In one of the cell blocks, the prisoners begin a riot to protest Stevens' death. Wilson orders the prisoners out of their cells and confronts them so decisively and effectively that only Joe Roberts and Jacko King still refuse to be pacified or intimidated. Together, they demand their right to file a formal protest against Williams. The two of them, despite attempts by both Wilson and Williams to dissuade them, are allowed to make a Statement to the Commandant. Before they have a chance to make their complaint, however, Williams and several other cell guards beat Roberts, who must be taken to the Medical Officer. The Medical Officer, who is now aroused to a sense of humanity, decides to send Roberts to the hospital; Wilson resists this because he fears the repurcussions if Roberts is allowed to make his statement outside prison confines. Jacko, infuriated, declares his resignation from the service, tears off his uniform and, clad only in his shorts, defiantly struts into the Commandant's office.

Williams, in a desperate effort to prevent the certain investigation of the Stevens incident, finds Roberts alone in the cell. Since Roberts is immobilized because of a broken ankle, Williams prepares to kill him. As he is about to do so, Jacko and McGrath also enter the cell and, realizing what is about to happen, brutally attack Williams. While Roberts vainly tries to stop them, Williams is presumably beaten to death, making the future prospects for reform and justice more hopeless than before.

Credits

Producer:	Kenneth Hyman
Director:	Sidney Lumet
Screenplay:	Ray Rigby, based on a play by Rigby and R. S. Allen
Photography:	Oswald Morris
Art Direction:	Herbert Smith
Music:	None
Sound Editor:	Peter Musgrave
Sound Recordist:	David Bowen
Recording Supervisor:	A. W. Watkins
Dubbing Mixer:	Fred Turtle
Film Editor:	Thelma Connell
Associate Producer:	Ray Anzarut
Assistant Directors:	Frank Ernst and Pedro Vidal
Make-up:	George Partleton
Wardrobe Supervisor:	Elsa Fennell
Technical Advisor:	George Montford
Camera Operator:	Brian West
Continuity:	Lee Turner
Cast:	Sean Connery (Joe Roberts), Harry Andrews (Regimental Sergeant Major Wilson), Ian Bannen (Harris), Alfred Lynch (George Stevens), Ossie Davis (Jacko King), Roy Kinnear (Monty Bartlett), Jack Watson (Jock McGrath),

Ian Hendry (Williams), Sir Michael Redgrave (Medical Officer), Norman Bird (Commandant), Neil McCarthy (Burton), Howard Goorney (Walters), Tony Caunter (Martin).

Filmed in London and on location in southern Spain
Distribution: MGM
Running Time: 123 minutes
Release: October, 1967

Note

At the Cannes Film Festival, the film won awards for best script *(ex-aequo)* and best director *(ex-aequo)*. The British Film Academy awarded it the prize for best black-and-white cinematography.

10 THE GROUP (1966)

This film follows the interacting lives of eight Vassar women, known as "The Group," during the half decade after their graduation. Graduating in 1933, the world promises optimism, hope and energy for the girls. In her valedictory address, Helena (Widdoes) tells the class, "This is the time that asks the woman of the world to play a roll in every sphere."

Lakey (Bergen), who has majored in art history, is intelligent, reserved and beautiful. She is the leader of the group and after graduation leaves for an extended stay in Europe. Kay (Pettet), with an interest in theater, is the first of the group to wed. She marries Harald (Hagman), an aspiring playwright. Because of the Depression, Kay takes a menial job at Macy's to help support Harald and his work. Harald, succumbing to his weaknesses for liquor and women, eventually loses his job as a stage manager. Later, Kay and Harald experience a violent breakup and Kay suffers from a nervous breakdown. At Kay's wedding, Dottie (Hackett), the oldest of the group and a wealthy Bostonian, meets the impoverished and disillusioned painter, Dick Brown (Mulligan). Seeking her first sexual adventure, she goes to a birth control clinic for contraceptives. Arranging to meet him in the park, he abandons her by never showing up. Humiliated and heartbroken, she returns to Boston. Priss (Hartman), a Phi Beta Kappa in economics and a political liberal, wants to work for President Roosevelt's NRA poverty program. The program is labelled illegal. She later marries Sloan (Cogdon), a domineering pediatrician, and after two miscarriages gives birth to a boy. Sloan is obsessed with the value of breast-feeding over bottle-feeding and although Priss has always been frail she reluctantly agrees. She is left exhausted and physically weak from the ordeal. Polly (Knight), a nurse, is the most basic of the group; she is conservative, sensitive and always ready to help. She goes to work at a hospital and has a brief affair with Gus Leroy (Holbrook), a sincere but weak-willed publisher. She tries to console and comfort him during his extended psychoanalysis but the relationship soon ends. Polly gradually finds a satisfying relationship with a dynamic young psychiatrist (Broderick). Her father (Emhardt), a manic-depressive, moves in with her and the doctor helps Polly cope with him. Helena, daughter of a steel magnate and the class valedictorian, wants to teach nursery school. Her wealthy socialite parents will not allow this so she spends her time travelling, entertaining and collecting art. Libby (Walter), the busy-body of the group who was once described by Lakey as having "a big red scar on her face called a mouth," is hypocritical, deceitful and egocentric. By connivery she becomes a professional success in New York's literary scene. Dispite her many stories of romantic conquests, she is emotionally insecure and sexually frigid. Pokey (Redd), also from a wealthy family, is easy-going. She eventually marries and settles down to an uncomplicated life, giving birth to two sets of twins.

In 1939, Lakey must return from Europe because war seems imminent. The other members of the group meet her at the port as she arrives with a very masculine looking Baroness (Prochnicka), her companion and lover. Dottie, still stifled by the memory of her Greenwich Village infatuation, is now unhappily married with two children. It is Dottie who gives a celebration party for Polly when she becomes engaged to the doctor. All the group members are there but Kay, who, since Harald's maltreatment and abandonment, has become preoccupied with the impending war. During the party they hear of Hitler's invasion of Holland and Belgium. Concerned about Kay's stability after her breakdown, Polly phones Kay, who has also heard the news. Thinking she hears enemy planes approaching, Kay leans too far out her window and falls to her death. The rest gather for her funeral, where Harald mysteriously reappears. On the way to the cemetery, Harald lashes out at Lakey's lesbianism.

Credits

Producer:	Sidney Buchman
Director:	Sidney Lumet
Screenplay:	Sidney Buchman, based on the novel by Mary McCarthy
Photography:	Boris Kaufman
Scenic Artist:	Stanley Cappiello
Production Designer:	Gene Callahan
Set Decoration:	Jack Wright, Jr.
Music Supervisor:	Charles Gross
Music Conducted by:	Robert deCormier
Sound:	Jack Fitzstephens and Dennis Maitland
Costumes:	Anna Hill Johnstone
Editor:	Ralph Rosenbloom
Production Manager:	Mel Howard
Production Supervisor:	Henry Spitz

Assistant Director:	Dan Eriksen, Tony Belletier
Make-up:	Irving Buchman
Hairstyles:	Frederick Jones
Cast:	Candice Bergen (Elinor Eastlake, "Lakey"), Joan Hackett (Dorothy Renfrew), Elizabeth Hartman (Priss Harshorn), Shirley Knight (Polly Andrews), Joanna Pettet (Kay Strong), Mary-Robin Redd (Pokey Prothero), Jessica Walter (Libby MacAusland), Kathleen Widdoes (Helena Davison), James Broderick (Dr. James Ridgeley), James Congdon (Sloan Crockett), Larry Hagman (Harald Peterson), Hal Holbrook (Gus Leroy), Richard Mulligan (Dick Brown), Robert Emhardt (Mr. Andrews), Carrie Nye (Norine), Philippa Bevans (Mrs. Hartshorn), Leta Bonynge (Mrs. Prothero), Marion Brash (Radio Man's Wife), Sara Burton (Mrs. Davison), Flora Campbell (Mrs. MacAusland), Bruno DiCosmi (Nils), Leora Dana (Mrs. Renfrew), Bill Fletcher (Bill), George Gaynes (Brook Latham), Martha Greenhouse (Mrs. Bergler), Russell Hardie (Mr. Davison), Doreen Lang (Nurse Swenson), Chet London (Radio Man), John O'Liary (Putnam Blake), Baruch Lumet (Mr. Schneider), Hildy Parks (Nurse Catherine), Lidia Prochnicka (The Baroness), Polly Rowles (Mrs. Andrews), Douglas Rutherford (Mr. Prothero), Truman Smith (Mr. Bergler), Loretta White (Mrs. Eastlake), Richard Graham (Rev. Garland), Arthur Anderson (Pokey's Husband), Clay Johns (Phil), Ed Holmes (Mr. MacAusland).
Filmed in New York	
Distribution:	United Artists
Running Time:	150 minutes
Color:	DeLuxe
Release:	March, 1966

11 THE DEADLY AFFAIR (1967)

Samuel Fennan (Flemyng), a top British Foreign Office official who is anonymously denounced as a Communist, commits suicide shortly after a security check has cleared him of the charge. Charles Dobbs (Mason), the Control Agent who conducted the security check, is baffled by the apparent irrationality of Fennan's death. Although Fennan left a typed suicide note saying that his career had been ruined by paid informers, Dobbs believes Fennan was actually murdered.

When orders instruct Dobbs to close the case, Dobbs resigns his post to find the murderer. With the help of a semi-retired CID officer, Inspector Mendel (Andrews), who is noticeably uncomfortable in the tangled world of Intelligence, Dobbs continues his investigation. Dobbs and Mendel question Fennan's wife, Elsa (Signoret), who is an embittered Jewish victim of

Nazi concentration camps. They catch Elsa in a lie about a telephone call and also discover that the anonymous denunciation letter and suicide note were typed on the same typewriter. Although Dobbs is aggressive in his work, he is passive in his marriage. In their destructive relationship, his wife, Ann (Anderson), claims to be compulsively driven to other men.

Meanwhile, Dieter Frey (Schell), an old friend of Dobbs from the war, arrives in London from Zurich, ostensibly to do business for a candy firm. Dobbs is distressed to find that his promiscuous wife is seducing Dieter and planning to leave with him. Dobbs and Mendel continue their investigation, which leads them to a run-down garage in a slum district in London and an office building, all of which eventually lead back to Elsa. Dobbs suggests that Fennan, who had discovered that his wife is a Communist agent and the security leak, had to be silenced. Dobbs now suspects that Dieter Frey is behind the entire operation. He and Mendel work out a plan to trap Elsa and Dieter into exposing themselves by meeting in a theatre during a performance of "Edward II."

Dieter, realizing he is being trapped, kills Elsa and in the confusion escapes. He is pursued by Dobbs and Mendel, who catch up with him at a houseboat in Chelsea. Dieter kills Mendel but hesitates to kill his old friend Dobbs. Taking advantage of the hesitation, Dobbs overcomes Dieter, who falls into the river and is crushed between the bank and the houseboat. Dobbs then flies to Zurich, where Ann has arranged to meet Dieter.

Credits

Producer:	Sidney Lumet
Director:	Sidney Lumet
Screenplay:	Paul Dehn, based on the novel *Call the Dead* by John Le Carre
Photography:	Freddie Young
Art Direction:	John Howell
Set Decorations:	Pamela Cornell
Music:	Quincy Jones
Theme Song, "Who Needs Forever," sung by:	Astrud Gilberto
Sound:	Les Hammond
Costumes:	Cynthia Tingay
Editor:	Thelma Connell
Associate Producer:	Denis O'Dell
Production Manager:	Victor Peck
Assistant Director:	Ted Sturgis
Make-up:	Jill Carpenter
Hairstyles:	Betty Glasgow
Cast:	James Mason (Charles Dobbs), Simone Signoret (Elsa Fennan), Maximilian Schell (Dieter Frey), Harriet Ander-

son (Ann Dobbs), Harry Andrews (Inspector Mendel), Kenneth Haigh (Bill Appleby), Lynn Redgrave (Virgin), Roy Kinnear (Adam Scarr), Max Adrian (Adviser), Robert Flemyng (Samuel Fennan), Colin Redgrave (Director), Les White (Harek), June Murphy, Frank Williams, Rosemary Lord (The Three Witches in "Macbeth"), Kenneth Ives (Stagehand), John Dimech (Waiter), Julian Sherrier (Head Waiter), Petra Markham (Daughter at Theatre), Denis Shaw (Landlord), Maria Charles (Blonde), Amanda Walker (Brunette), Sheraton Blout (Eunice Scarr), Janet Hargreaves (Ticket Clerk), Michael Brennan (Barman), Richard Steele and Gartan Klauber (Businessmen), Margaret Lacey (Mrs. Bird), Judy Keirn (Stewardess), and The Royal Shakespeare Company in "Edward II" by Christopher Marlowe, directed by Peter Hall: David Warner (King Edward), Michael Bryant (Gaveston), Stanley Leber (Lancaster), Paul Hardwick (Young Mortimer), Charles Kay (Lightborn), Timothy West (Matrevis), Jonathan Hales (Gurney), William Dysart, Murray Brown, Paul Starr, Peter Harrison, David Quilter, Terence Sewards and Roger Jones (Nobles).

Filmed on location in London
Distribution: BLC/Columbia
Running Time: 107 minutes
Color: Technicolor
Release: February, 1967

12 BYE, BYE BRAVERMAN (1968)

One Sunday morning in New York, Morroe (Segal) is called by Inez (Walter), the wife of his good friend Leslie Braverman. She tells Morroe that Leslie is dead. Shocked to hear of the premature death of the young intellectual writer, Morroe, against the wishes of his wife, Etta (Lampert), goes to see Inez. Trying to forget that Leslie owed him money, Morroe arrives at Inez's house, where, to his surprise, she tries to seduce him.

Morroe calls three of Leslie's closest friends, all fellow writers, and arranges to meet them in Greenwich Village to attend the funeral. Barnet Weiner (Warden) lives on the Lower East Side. His mistress, Myra Mandelbaum (Newman), stays with him Saturday nights and Sunday mornings. Myra, who lounges around in scanty underthings, is beautiful and intelligent (she has studied psychology). She calls Barnet a "mad bastard with fake sociology." Barnet wears a red toupee, which he removes immediately upon hearing bad news. Felix Ottensteen (Wiseman) is the oldest of the four. He was born speaking Yiddish and identifies so closely with God that he sometimes carries on conversations with Him as a peer. He is very moral, honest and stingy. Felix has just had a spat with his poet-son, Max (Holland), who wanted money. Felix refused, slapped his son and then asked God why He took Leslie instead of Max. He tells his son, "I wasn't crazy about your mother, but I like you even less." Holly Levine (Booke), fat and bald, is the most commercially successful of the four. Before writing, he proceeds through a ritual of procrastination: sharpening pencils, cleaning his desk, fiddling with a giant cigarette lighter. He is preparing to type an article in his Greenwich Village apartment, which is filled with Pop Art, posters and oddities. To get away from his typewriter, he offers to drive them all to the funeral.

Morroe, Barnet, Felix and Holly meet in Greenwich Village and pile into Holly's shiny, new red Volkswagen. It takes some coaxing to get Felix into a German-made care ("This legacy from Hitler") but he is finally persuaded. The four head for the funeral, which is to be held somewhere in Brooklyn. The friends talk about everything but only occasionally mention Leslie; he is called "A second-rate talent of the highest order" by one. On the way to Brooklyn, they have an accident with a black cab driver (Cambridge). The driver almost starts a fight, but then he tells them he is also Jewish, an evangelistic convert, and after a monologue on tolerance, the harsh feelings are softened and eventually a bottle of wine is passed around. The four friends leave, noticeably tipsy. They finally reach the synagogue and sit through a lengthy eulogy, believing the service to be for Leslie. Holly is hungry, Felix is serious, and Morroe and Barnet veer between weeping and laughing at the rabbi's (King) eccentric comments. To their astonishment they discover that they are at the wrong synagogue and the service is not for Leslie but for someone named Morris. Deciding whether or not they have grieved enough for one day, they plod on and finally reach Leslie's grave. At the crowded cemetery, Morroe delivers a soliloquy on the sad state of the world: cinema, economics, kitsch, death, pollution, medicine, crime, marriage and government. He tells the tombstones, "If doctors had done better, they could have kept some of you alive longer." After a moment of reflection, he adds, "I don't think you missed much." That night, as Morroe tells his wife the happenings of his day, he begins to weep.

Interspersed throughout his odyssey, Morroe fantasizes events in his own projected death: from seeing himself as a policeman breaking the news of his death to a woman to digging his own grave and burying himself.

Credits

Producer:	Sidney Lumet
Director:	Sidney Lumet
Screenplay:	Herbert Sargent, based on the novel *To An Early Grave* by Wallace Markfield
Photography:	Boris Kaufman
Art Direction:	Ben Kasazkow
Set Decorations:	John Godfrey
Music:	Peter Matz
Sound:	Dick Vorisek
Costumes:	Anna Hill Johnstone

Editor:	Ralph Rosenblum
Associate Producer:	Charles Maguire
Production Supervisor:	Kenneth Utt
Assistant Directors:	Burtt Harris and Alan Hopkins
Production Assistant:	Fred C. Caruso
Cast:	George Segal (Morroe Rieff), Jack Warden (Barnet Weiner), Jessica Walter (Inez Braverman), Phyllis Newman (Myra Mandelbaum), Godfrey Cambridge (Taxi Cab Driver), Joseph Wiseman (Felix Ottensteen), Sorrell Booke (Holly Levine), Zohra Lampert (Etta Rieff), Anthony Holland (Max Ottensteen), Susan Wyler (Pilar), Lieb Lensky (Custodian), Alan King (The Rabbi).
Filmed on location in New York	
Distribution:	Warner Brothers - Seven Arts
Running Time:	94 minutes
Color:	Technicolor
Release:	April, 1968

13   THE SEA GULL (1968)

This film is a faithful screen version of Anton Chekhov's play, set in late nineteenth century Russia. Arkadina (Signoret) is a famous actress. She is self-centered, vain, and wants to forget she is old enough to have a son in his twenties. Arkadina is visiting her brother, Sorin (Andrews), a retired official, at his country house for a long weekend. She is with her lover, Trigorin (Mason), a famous novelist. Konstantin (Warner), Arkadina's son, is a writer, but Arkadina feels his work is absurd and does not pay much attention to it. Konstantin is in love with Nina (Redgrave), the daughter of a neighbor. He is distressed by Trigorin's presence, since Trigorin's charm has captivated Nina's attention. Because of this and the others laughing at his play, Konstantin attempts suicide. He places a dead sea gull at Nina's feet and tells her that one day he too will be dead. Also there for the weekend is Sorin's bailiff, Shamraev (Radd), his wife Polina (Herlie), his daughter Masha (Widdoes) and a doctor (Elliott). Masha, in love with Konstantin, shows her hopeless feelings by wearing black, drinking too much, and taking snuff in front of the others. Medvedenko (Lynch), a schoolmaster, is in love with Masha.

Arkadina and Trigorin return to Moscow after their visit. Nina arranges to meet Trigorin in Moscow and becomes his mistress. Trigorin leaves Nina after she bears him a stillborn son. She then attempts to become an actress but is not very successful.

Two years later, Arkadina and Trigorin go back to Sorin's estate. We find Masha has married Medvedenko but is unhappy. Konstantin has had success with his writings. Nina says that she still loves Trigorin. After this news, Konstantin shoots himself while the others are playing cards.

Credits

Producer:	Sidney Lumet
Director:	Sidney Lumet
Screenplay:	Technical Advisor and Translation by Mour Budberg of the play by Anton Chekhov
Photography:	Gerry Fisher, B.S.C.
Camera Operator:	Anders Bodin, F.S.F.
Scenic Artist:	Eric Bjork
Set Decorations:	Rune Hjelm and Rolf Larsson
Sound Recordist:	Leslie Hammond
Costumes:	Tony Walton
Editor:	Alan Heim
Production Design:	Tony Walton
Associate Producer:	F. Sherwin Green
Production Manager:	Ronald Sundberg
Assistant Director:	Waldemar Bergendahl
Make-up:	Tina Johansson and Kjell Gustavsson
Wardrobe:	Eve Faloon, Maj Erikson
Hairstyles:	Tina Johansson and Kjell Gustavsson
Continuity:	Inga-Lisa Britz
Design Assistants:	Lennart Clemens, Philip Rosenberg
Publicist:	Carl Combs
Cast:	James Mason (Trigorin), Vanessa Redgrave (Nina), Simone Signoret (Arkadina), David Warner (Konstantin), Harry Andrews (Sorin), Denholm Elliott (Dorn), Eileen Herlie (Polina), Alfred Lynch (Medvedenko), Ronald Radd (Shamraev), Kathleen Widdoes (Masha), Frej Lindquest (Yakov), Karen Miller (Housemaid).
Filmed on location in Sweden and at Europa Studios Stockholm	
Distribution:	Seven Arts
Running Time:	141 minutes
Color:	Technicolor
Release:	December, 1968

14 THE APPOINTMENT (1969)

Federico Fendi (Sharif) is a young and successful lawyer in Rome. He tells us, "I was in the summer of my life . . . I could see myself changing."

One day while driving along the streets of Rome, he is fascinated by a mysterious and beautiful woman (Aimee) among the pedestrians on the sidewalk. He follows her for a short distance but loses her in the crowd. At lunch with a colleague who is also an old schoolfriend, Renzo (Tozzi), they are joined by Carla, the woman he had seen earlier. Federico discovers that she is engaged to Renzo. Later, Federico meets her again as she is walking on the street. She is distressed and asks Federico to help her discover why Renzo has broken off their engagement. Federico meets Renzo for lunch. Renzo explains that his cousin from Milan had patronized an exclusive brothel while visiting in Rome; the cousin had stolen an attractive pin, a gold seahorse, from the prostitute and given it to his wife as a present. Renzo claims that he recognized the pin as one he had previously given to Carla. He further explains that, when questioned, Carla said she had lost the pin. Renzo has broken off the engagement because he believes Carla to be the prostitute.

Federico then tells Carla that Renzo had decided to marry another woman; Federico does not mention the pin or the incident to her. Carla is terribly distraught and Federico takes her home. Becoming increasingly obsessed with Carla, Federico goes to Milan to interview Renzo's cousin about his visit to the brothel, but he only says, "I'm sorry, I can't be of any help." Back in Rome, Federico and Renzo discuss a litigation case over lunch. Renzo informs Federico that he knows of his trip to Milan, but Renzo adds that Federico can only find the answer to his investigation at a certain address, which he gives to Federico. Federico proceeds to the address, a Decorator's Shop, where he coyly baits the proprietess (Lenya): "I was informed that one could have quite a pleasant time." She tells him that she will try to arrange a meeting.

Federico and Carla's involvement mutually grows, but Federico continues to keep his suspicions and investigation a secret from her. Several days later, he returns to the shop where he is assigned to meet the mysterious prostitute he believes to be Carla. The woman is not Carla, and he is temporarily reassured. His persistent doubts eventually compel him back to the shop, however, where he continues his quest for the woman, "the kind of girl one wouldn't expect to find working in a place like this." He and the proprietess arrange another appointment, but she must wait for the woman to call her. Federico and Carla spend an idyllic weekend on a picturesque Mediterranean island. Her hesitation to consummate their relationship disturbs Federico. In bitterness at his rejection, he returns to his office in Rome. The shop keeper calls about the woman. Federico goes to the shop, where he expects to confront the woman he still believes to be Carla, but she does not appear.

Federico is notified that Carla is in the hospital, having taken an overdose of sleeping pills. Carla's gesture renews Federico's faith in her. When she is released from the hospital, the two return to their Mediterranean resort, where they are passionate and happy. Federico and Renzo meet as opposing attorneys in the separation case. Through a series of innuendoes, Renzo rekindles Federico's suspicions about Carla. A series of events (Carla's lie about "the dentist" and her disturbance over a "wrong number") force Federico back to the shop keeper, who has arranged the appointment for Federico to meet the woman. Again no one appears. But Carla, depressed by Federico's antagonistic behavior, again takes an overdose of pills and dies at the hospital. A final phone call from the shop keeper informs Federico that the woman is "still interested."

Credits

Producer:	Martin Poll
Director:	Sidney Lumet
Screenplay:	James Salter, from an original story by Antonio Leonviola
Photography:	Carlo Di Palma
Art Direction:	Piero Gherardi
Set Dresser:	Arrigo Breschi
Music:	John Barry
Additional Music and Orchestration:	Don Walker
Sound:	David Hildyard
Wardrobe:	Alda Marussig
Film Editor:	Thelma Connell
Production Supervisor:	Orazio Tassara
Make-up:	Otello Fava
Hair Stylist:	Renata Magnanti
Props:	Lamberto Verdenelli
Cast:	Omar Sharif (Federico Fendi), Anouk Aimee (Carla), Lotte Lenya (Emma Valandier), Paola Barbara (Mother), Didi Perego (Nany), Luigi Proiette (Fabre), Fausto Tozzi (Renzo), Inna Alexeieff (Old Woman on Train), Ennio Balbo (Ugo Perino), Linda De Felice (Fisherman's Wife), Sandro Dori (Cutter), Cyrus Elias (Apprentice Lawyer), Gabriella Grimaldi (Anna), Isabella Guidotti (Perino's Secretary), Angelo Infanti (Antonio), M. Grazia Marescalchi (Mrs. Delfini), Serena Michelotti (Lucia), Nerina Montagnani (Head Seamstress), Germana Paolieri (Maid), Monica Pardo (Olghina).
Filmed on location in Rome	
Distribution:	Metro
Running time:	100 minutes
Color:	Metrocolor
Release:	1969

15 KING: A FILMED RECORD . . . MONTGOMERY TO MEMPHIS
(1969)

This film was made for a single nationwide performance on March 24, 1969 in one thousand selected theatres, the proceeds to be donated to the King Fund. John Goff in his review of the film for *Hollywood Reporter* observed that it "is not so much a motion picture than a painful chronicling of heart-breaking, head-busting, back-splitting events clothed in anguish, bathed in blood and tears, urged on by death, desire and determination which were nurtured, fed and given strength by the eloquence, dreams and love of a single man — Martin Luther King Jr."

The film covers the rise of the civil rights movement in the United States from 1955 to 1968, "reviving its tempered pursuit of idealistic adversary, and freezing it as a prelude to polarization instead of harmony" according to Barry Glasser in *The Motion Picture Herald*. The film opens with a juxtaposition of black militant rhetoric and King's articulation of his non-violent policy ("I am sick and tired of violence"). The emphasis is on King as a public figure, growing in stature and confidence from a shy, youthful minister in 1955 to a charismatic moral visionary. It is a non-narrated film using authentic footage which is mobilized to document this important period.

The film follows King through: Montgomery and the Bus Boycott in 1955 where he was arrested; the Freedom Rides in the early sixties where he tells his followers, "The minute you conquer the fear of death, you're free"; the March on Washington where he delivers his "I have a dream" speech; the Atrocities of Birmingham, St. Augustine, Selma, and Chicago which resulted in the Civil Rights Act of 1965; the Nobel Peace Prize; his appearance in Chicago in July of 1966 where he leads his followers on a march to Mayor Daley's home, warning, "If you don't help me, you're opening the door to letting violence take over"; the Poor People's Campaign; and finally his assassination and funeral in Memphis in 1968, where there is a voice-over recording of the sermon in which he predicts his own death and claims that he wants to be remembered not for his honors but for his struggles.

Interspersed throughout the film are brief, contemporary commentaries by such celebrities as Harry Belafonte, Ben Gazzara, Clarence Williams III, Paul Newman, Joanne Woodward, Ruby Dee, Burt Lancaster, Charlton Heston, Sidney Poitier, James Earl Jones and Anthony Quinn reciting from the writings of Ralph Ellison, Ernest Hemingway, Dick Gregory, Langston Hughes and the *Bible* to establish the emotional context of the period covered. (This was the section of the film that Lumet and Mankiewicz directed.

"This is indeed the stuff of topical drama, complete with burning crosses, police dogs, strident white backlash and such instantly recognizable heavies as southern sheriffs 'Bull' Conner and Jim Clarke — no less frightening personages for epitomizing the bullish stereotypes which come out of Central Casting" (Verr. in *Variety*).

Credits

Producer:	Ely Landau
Directors of connecting sequences:	Sidney Lumet and Joseph L. Mankiewicz
Associate Producer:	Richard Kaplan
Editing Staff Headed by:	Lora Hays and John Carter
Distribution:	Maron
Running Time:	153 minutes
Release:	September, 1969

Note

The film collected an Academy Award nomination for best documentary.

16 LAST OF THE MOBILE HOT-SHOTS (1970)

Jeb Thorington (Coburn), thrown out of a New Orleans bar, wanders into *The Rube Benedict Show,* where "Happy Couple Time" is being aired on television. For $35,000 and a truckload of appliances, he marries Myrtle (Redgrave), a total stranger, on the program.

Immediately after the ceremony, they leave for Jeb's ancestral home, "Waverly Plantation." Because of years of impoverishment and neglect, Waverly, a once lavish Southern plantation, has deteriorated. Jeb, who is dying of cancer, desperately wants a son to prevent his half-brother, Chicken (Hooks), from inheriting the estate. Myrtle, a vivacious but shallow red-head who aspires toward showbusiness, had been a member of a topless band called "The Five Hot-Shots from Mobile." Upon reaching Waverly, Jeb confines himself to his upstairs bedroom, where he lives on the memories of Waverly's past greatness. He is also haunted by the memory of an incident in which he and Chicken shared two prostitutes; during the encounter, Jeb finds himself impotent and painfully watches Chicken and the two women from a corner. To console himself for his present suffering, Jeb is now dependent on marijuana.

Upon meeting Chicken, Myrtle finds him to be uncivil and unforgiving. Myrtle finds out that Chicken is actually half black. Jeb believes that he and Chicken had different mothers, "Different as night and day," but the same father; however, it is revealed that they had the same mother but different fathers. This becomes legally important because Waverly was owned by the mother and must by law be left to her next blood kin. The two half-brothers become bitter rivals over the legacy of Waverly. Jeb convinces Myrtle to trick Chicken into handing over a document that would make him the heir upon Jeb's death. Because of Jeb's impotence and her sexual appetite, she succumbs to Chicken's advances.

News of an impending flood threatens the lives and property of Waverly. Jeb, in one last desperate attempt to force the inheritance document from Chicken, descends from his bedroom with an old Civil War revolver but, before he can use it, collapses from exhaustion and dies. The flood comes, and Chicken and Myrtle climb to the roof of the delapidated mansion, which is the only place of safety.

Credits

Producer:	Sidney Lumet
Director:	Sidney Lumet
Screenplay:	Gore Vidal, based on *The Seven Descents of Myrtle* by Tennessee Williams as produced on stage by David Merrick
Photography:	James Wong Howe
Set Decoration:	Leif B. Pedersei
Production Design:	Gene Callahan
Music:	Quincy Jones
Sound:	Nat Boxer
Recording Mixer:	Richard Vorisek
Costume Design:	P. Zipprodt
Editor:	Alan Heim
Assistant Directors:	Burtt Harris, Bob Brand
Associate Producer:	Jim DiGangi
Hair Stylist:	F. Jones
Publicist:	Jim Merrick
Cast:	James Coburn (Jeb), Lynn Redgrave (Myrtle), Robert Hooks (Chicken), Perry Hayes (George), Reggie King (Rube).
Distribution:	Warner Brothers
Running Time:	108 minutes
Color:	Technicolor
Release:	January, 1970
British Title:	*Blood Kin*

17 THE ANDERSON TAPES (1971)

Professional safe cracker Duke Anderson (Connery) is released, feeling bitter and hostile, after a ten-year prison sentence. He goes to the Manhattan luxury apartment (at 1 East 91st Street) of Engrid Everleigh (Cannon), his former mistress. Unknown to them both, her apartment has been bugged by her wealthy but possessive lover, Werner (Schull), who wants to insure his exclusivity. Anderson sees her building as a good potential robbery. "I'm going to back up a van and steal the guts out of the whole place," he tells her.

Anderson convinces two fellow ex-cons to help him. The Kid (Walken) is an electronics expert who was jailed for a drug offence and is now under surveillance by the Narcotics Division. Pop (Gottlieb), frightened by his freedom after thirty-five years in prison, agrees to the heist. Anderson also gets three other men. Tommy Haskins (Balsam) is a homosexual antique dealer whose phone is being tapped because the government thinks he is fencing fake antiques. Tommy, acting as the "bird dog," is to appraise and mark the items of value in the building. Jimmy (Benjamin) and Spencer (Williams) are to be the getaway drivers. Spencer is a black truck driver and is being watched because he lives in the same building as some Black Panthers. For financial backing, Anderson goes to Pat Angelo (King), a Mafia boss. Angelo is being bugged by the Internal Revenue. Angelo, excited at the prospects of an "old time caper," agrees to back Anderson under the condition that he take one of his gunmen, Socks Parelli (Avery) and kill him during the robbery. The agreement is made and arrangements are finalized to rob the building on Labor Day, when most of the tenants will be away. All the investigating agencies are working independently; no one seems to be interested in Anderson.

On the day of the robbery, the men back a large moving van into the driveway of the apartment building. Pop takes the doorman's post and monitors the closed-circuit television system. The Kid disconnects the security alarm and the rest begin to loot the apartments, taking the marked items. As they systematically cover the building they imprison the tenants. The mistake is made when they enter the Bingham apartment. Mr. and Mrs. Bingham (Showalter, Ward) are put with the other tenants, but their paraplegic son, Jerry (Jacoby), is allowed to remain alone in his bedroom. Jerry is an electronics buff and, using his ham radio, reports the robbery to the police. Unknown to the robbers, the building is surrounded by hordes of police, headed by Captain Delaney (Meeker). Delaney cordons off the street and puts one of his men in the lobby as others are working their way through an adjoining building. Hearing the footsteps of the approaching police, Anderson orders his men to lock the stairwells and head downstairs to the waiting van. Tommy Haskins and Pop have given themselves up. During the ensuing struggle, Anderson is fatally shot. The rest are either captured or killed as they try to escape.

When the news of the attempted robbery is made public, the various investigation agencies decide to destroy all tapes in which Anderson is mentioned so that their extra-legal activities will not be discovered.

Credits

Producer:	Robert M. Weitman
Director:	Sidney Lumet
Screenplay:	Frank R. Pierson, based on the novel by Lawrence Sanders
Photography:	Arthur J. Ornitz
Art Direction:	Philip Rosenberg
Set Decoration:	Alan Hicks
Music Composed and Conducted by:	Quincy Jones

Sound:	Dennis Maitland, Jack Fitzstephens and Al Gramaglia
Costumes:	Gene Coffin
Editor:	Joanne Burke
Production Design:	Benjamin J. Kasazkrow
Assistant Director:	Alan Hopkins
Associate Producer:	George Justin
Make-up:	Saul Meth
Hairstyles:	Ian Forrest and Betty Destefano
Casting:	Marion Dougherty
Cast:	Sean Connery (Duke Anderson), Dyan Cannon (Ingrid Everleigh), Martin Balsam (Tommy Haskins), Ralph Meeker (Captain Delaney), Alan King (Pat Angelo), Christopher Walker (The Kid), Val Avery (Socks Parelli), Dick Williams (Spencer), Garrett Morris (Everson), Stan Gottlieb (Pop), Paul Benjamin (Jimmy), Anthony Holland (Psychologist), Conrad Bain (Dr. Rubicoff), Richard B. Schull (Werner), Margaret Hamilton (Miss Kaler), Judith Lowry (Mrs. Hathaway), Max Showalter (Bingham), Janet Ward (Mrs. Bingham), Scott Jacoby (Jerry Bingham), Norman Rose (Longene), Med Miles (Mrs. Longene), Ralph Stanley (D'Medico), John Call (O'Leary), John Bradon (Vanessi), Paula Trueman (Nurse), Michael Miller (First Agent), Michael Prince (Johnson), Frank Macetta (Papa Angelo), Jack Doroshow (Eric), Michael Clary (Eric's Friend), Hildy Brook (Receptionist), Robert Dagny (Doctor), Bradford English (TV Watcher), Reid Cruckshanks (Judge), Tom Signorelli (Sync Man), Carmine Caridi (Detective A), Michael Fairman (Sgt. Claire), Philip Larson (Policeman), Charles Frank (Medic), George Patelis (Detective B), William Da Prato (Detective C), Sam Coppola (Private Detective).
Filmed on location in New York	
Distribution:	Columbia-Warner Brothers
Running Time:	98 minutes
Color:	Technicolor
Release:	June, 1971

18 CHILD'S PLAY (1972)

This film takes place almost entirely in St. Charles Roman Catholic Boarding School for Boys. As the film begins, we are taken on a tour of the school, with its empty hallways, classrooms, gymnasium, chapel and finally a dormitory with sleeping students. While some of the students hold another, they cut his finger and draw a cross in blood on his forehead.

Paul Reis (Bridges), who graduated from the school nine years ago, arrives at the school as the new physical education teacher. He is happily greeted by Joe Dobbs (Preston), his former and admired English teacher. Reis also meets the cynical Father Penny (Rounds). A student, Jennings (Fraser), talks to Dobbs about charges brought against him by his Latin teacher, Jerome Malley (Mason). Dobbs intercedes and asks Malley, called "Lash" by the students, to be lenient with Jennings; but Malley flatly refuses. Dobbs takes Reis on a tour of the school. They discuss Malley, who was supposed to retire this term after thirty years of teaching but has decided to stay on. Because of this, Dobbs could not be promoted to the head of the senior class. Their tour takes them to the gym, where Reis gives a demonstration of his ability on parallel bars. Soon, they hear fighting in the locker room. Reis hastens to see what the trouble is and finds a group of boys slamming a student's head against a locker. After the boys have gone, the student, Travis (Man), will not tell Reis who they were. Reis talks to Father Penny about the incident; Father Penny informs him that there have been six such student-caused "incidents" of "boys intending maximum physical hurt" in the past semester. The headmaster, Father Mozian (Weyand), will not do anything about these "accidents."

In Malley's Latin class, when a question of translation baffles most of the class, Freddy Banks (O'Keefe) reluctantly but correctly answers. Later, in the gym, Reis momentarily leaves Banks in charge while he leaves to get his stopwatch. When he returns after only a few minutes, the boys are beating Banks. Reis tries to help him, but Banks resists. Banks' eye is gouged out as a consequence. Father Mozian, believing Malley's harsh standards to be the source of the violence, calls Malley to his office and advises him "to ease up" on the boys. He shows Malley a derogatory note, presumably written by a student, and tells him that this obscene note is not the first. Malley tells him that Dobbs is the "malevolence" and accuses Dobbs of wanting the senior class. Dobbs and Reis visit Banks at the hospital, and Banks confesses that there is some kind of "agreement" among the boys but will not say what it is. Malley coincidentally meets Dobbs in the chapel where they express their mutual animosity. Malley accuses Dobbs of making obscene phone calls to his mother, who is dying of cancer. When they leave, several students sneak into the chapel; they beat, strip and tie a student to a cross in the chapel. After this incident, Father Mozian orders the chapel closed and all doors locked fifteen minutes after classes are over. When Malley's mother is taken to the hospital, Father Mozian suggests that he take a few days off. Malley goes to his office to pick up his mail and searches Dobbs' desk for the receipt for a subscription to a pornographic magazine that he believes Dobbs is having sent to him. Reis gradually becomes more responsive to Malley, as he gets to know him better. The hospital calls to tell Malley his mother has passed away. Malley tells Reis that this will make "him" (referring to Dobbs) happy.

Later that evening, as Reis is talking to Father Penny, someone throws a desecrated picture of Jesus at the door. Father Penny drops his glass and Reis intentionally cuts his hand. Dobbs enters and bandages Reis. Malley returns to the school before his leave days expire and is noticeably easier on the boys. At a meeting with Father Mozian he finds that his temporary replacement is to become permanent. Malley pleads with Father Mozian, promising to do anything, but Father Mozian says Malley must resign. Malley again tells Father Mozian about the magazines and phone calls, but Father Mozian does not believe him. Reis finds out that Malley has been forced to retire and pleads with Father Mozian. Dismayed, Malley jumps to his death from the roof of the school. Reis runs to Malley, accusing Dobbs, "Joe, come out and see what you've done."

The school is ordered closed for the next semester. Reis confronts Dobbs with his belief that Malley's accusations were true. Dobbs takes him downstairs where "the boys" of Dobbs' class wait. When Reis fails to convince them that Dobbs has manipulated their behavior, the boys (presumably) kill him. In the final scene, Dobbs is calmly sitting alone in the chapel. The boys arrive and ominously encircle him.

Credits

Producer:	David Merrick
Director:	Sidney Lumet
Screenplay:	Leon Prochnik, based on the play by Robert Marasco produced on the Broadway stage by David Merrick
Photography:	Gerald Hirschfield
Production Design:	Philip Rosenberg
Music Composed and Conducted by:	Michael Small
Sound:	William Edmondson
Costumes:	Ruth Morley
Make-up:	Saul Meth
Editors:	Edward Warschilka and Joanne Burke, A.C.
Wardrobe Supervisor:	George Newman
Associate Producer:	Hank Moonjean
Associate Director:	Hank Moonjean
Unit Production Manager:	Jim DiGangi
Script Supervisor:	Nick Sgarro
Casting Director:	Geri Windsor
Cast:	James Mason (Jerome Malley), Robert Preston (Joseph Dobbs), Beau Bridges (Paul Reis), Ronald Weyand (Father Mozian), Charles White (Father Griffin), David Rounds (Father Penny), Kate Harrington (Mrs. Carter), Jamie Alexander (Sheppard), Brian Chapin (O'Donnell), Bryant Fraser (Jennings), Mark Hall Haefeli (Wilson), Ton Leopold (Shea), Julius Lo Iacono (McArdle), Christopher

Man (Travis), Paul O'Keefe (Banks), Robert D. Randall (Medley), Robbie Reed (Class President), Paul Alessio, Anthony Barletta, Kevin Coupe, Christopher Hoag and Stephen McLaughlin (students).

Filmed on location at Marymount Secondary School and Tarrytown-on-the-Hudson, New York
Distribution: Paramount
Running Time: 100 minutes
Color: Movielab

19 THE OFFENCE (1973)

There is a child molester at large who has claimed three victims. Despite warnings from the police, a small schoolgirl, Janie Edmonds (Gordon), is accosted by an unidentified man and led into the woods bordering a play ground. That evening, Detective Sergeant Johnson (Connery) leads his men into the area to search for the missing girl. After an intensive search, Johnson discovers the fourth victim, who is in shock and repels him in fright. A city wide man-hunt for suspects is initiated by the police.

Soon, Baxter (Bannen) is picked up in a routine investigation and taken to police headquarters for questioning about the child. There is no real evidence that Baxter is in fact the child molester, but Johnson is intuitively convinced he is guilty. During an unauthorized private interrogation, Johnson beats Baxter savagely. Johnson must be restrained by his colleagues and is subsequently suspended from the force while Baxter is sent for emergency treatment at the hospital. During his drive home, Johnson recalls fragmentary images of violence, presumably from his past cases. After internalizing twenty years of police work it becomes obvious that Johnson is a man at the breaking point. He tries to share his feelings of agony and exhaustion with his wife, Maureen (Merchant), explaining how hard it is to deal with all the violence he has experienced. Johnson becomes enraged, verbally lacerating her for her lack of understanding and their marital unhappiness. Johnson learns that Baxter has died as a result of his beating. Under severe mental strain, he is ordered to go to police headquarters for questioning about Baxter's death.

Claiming that he was certain of Baxter's guilt, Johnson tells his superior officer, Cartwright (Howard), of the events which occurred on the day of the interrogation. Johnson tells (in a flashback) how he attempted to extract a confession from Baxter by sharing his own tormented thoughts of violent behavior. Baxter, we discover, was overcome by guilt — not because he was a child molester but because of his homosexuality, emergent after eighteen years of marriage. Baxter's torment ("I've waited all my life for God to punish me") outrages Johnson, who seems to harbor a latent homosexuality himself. Baxter, because of his own guilt feelings, recognizes a guilt in Johnson. Baxter ignites Johnson by telling him, "You sad, sorry little man . . . nothing I have done can be half as bad as the thoughts in your head. I wouldn't have your thoughts. Don't beat me for thoughts in your head, things you want to do . . . nothing I can, you haven't imagined." Johnson, incensed, brutally turns on Baxter because Baxter has brought him too dangerously close to the truth about himself.

During the questioning, Johnson has unconsciously betrayed his own psychopathic inclinations to Cartwright. Cartwright, realizing in Johnson the destructive potential that can overcome a policeman who takes his job internally, can sympathize but cannot condone Johnson's action: "It makes me sick what you did, Johnson. What you are turns my stomach." Leaving Cartwright, Johnson begins to fully perceive what he has done and become.

Credits

Producer:	Denis O'Dell
Director:	Sidney Lumet
Screenplay:	John Hopkins, based on his play *This Story of Yours*
Photography:	Gerry Fisher
Art Direction:	John Clark
Music:	Harrison Birtwhistle
Sound:	Simon Kaye
Costumes:	Vangie Harrison
Editor:	John Victor Smith
Production Manager:	Victor Peck
Location Manager:	Barry Melrose
Assistant Director:	Ted Sturgis
Cast:	Sean Connery (Detective Sergeant Johnson), Trevor Howard (Cartwright), Vivien Merchant (Maureen Johnson), Ian Bannen (Baxter), Derek Newark (Jessard), John Hallam (Panton), Peter Bowles (Cameron), Ronald Radd (Lawson), Anthony Sagar (Hill), Howard Goorney (Lambeth), Richard Moore (Garrett), Maxine Gordon (Janie).
Filmed on location in London	
Distribution:	United Artists
Running Time:	113 minutes
Color:	DeLuxe
Release:	May, 1973

20 SERPICO (1974)

As the credits appear on the screen, the sound of a siren gradually rises. Shot in the face during a narcotics raid, Serpico (Pacino) is being rushed to the hospital. As he is in the police squad car, the film flashbacks to his graduation day at the Police Academy.

As a rookie police officer, Frank Serpico begins as a clean-cut idealist. He joins New York's 82nd Precinct and is almost immediately introduced to common but harmless gratuities, such as taking a free meal, as well as more flagrant abuses, such as the beating of a prisoner, and lack of co-operation in the department. Despite the petty corruption he finds, Serpico retains his youthful enthusiasm. Because it is supposed to be the quickest route toward a detective's position, Serpico requests to be transferred to the Fingerprint Identification Bureau. He is assigned routine clerical work but does not get along well with the others because of his unconventional attitudes and behavior. He grows a moustache and long hair, wears t-shirts and rides a motorcycle; he is called "a weirdo cop" by his co-workers. He is also taking classes at New York University, where he meets a dancer, Leslie Land (Sharpe).

Bored by his work, Serpico persuades Inspector McClain (McGuire) to transfer him to the 21st Precinct, where he begins to work as a plain-clothes patrolman on the streets. As an undercover officer he encounters gross negligence (two uniformed patrolmen, accidentally, nearly kill him) and is first offered pay-off money. Frustrated and confused, he turns to Bob Blair (Roberts), with whom he went through the academy and who is on the Mayor's special investigating committee. He tells Blair, "It's incredible. I feel like a criminal because I don't take money." He feels alienated and isolated from his co-workers because it seems that he alone resists the corruption that all the others accept as part of the job.

Leslie leaves Serpico. Soon he meets Laurie (Eda-Young), a nurse, and she moves in with him. Determined to preserve his honesty and yet not antagonize others, Serpico asks Inspector McClain again to transfer him. McClain does this and says that his new division is "clean as a hound's tooth." At the new precinct, to his disillusionment, Serpico finds he is under as much pressure to accept bribes and pay-offs as before. He privately reports this to McClain, who asks Serpico to secretly investigate the issue more fully for Commissioner Delaney (White). Pressure and harassment from his fellow officers "to take money" build, but Serpico impatiently waits. No official action is ever taken. Again he goes to Blair, and together they go to a friend who can supposedly get Mayoral action. This falls through when the Mayor refuses to act on the charges, fearing both unpopular publicity and the prospects of summer race riots. Eventually Delaney initiates an investigation, but Grand Jury hearings do not satisfy Serpico.

When it becomes known that Serpico is co-operating with an investigating committee, his colleagues begin to threaten his life. Under the constant strain imposed by his job, Serpico has now become obsessed and paranoid. His relationship with Laurie has deteriorated; Serpico abusively takes out his professional agonies on her. He complains, "If they'd take all that energy [that goes into collecting pay-offs] and put it into straight police work, they could clean up this city in a week." Laurie, who can neither appreciate nor help him, is finally driven away from him and leaves. Serpico and Blair find Captain Lombardo (Grover) to back them up, and together they go to the *New York Times* to tell their story of corruption. Serpico is very soon transferred to the Narcotics Division, while a special commission re-opens the inquiry. Captain Lombardo is convinced that "There are a lot of good cops out there who'd come forward if they had any encouragement." While the investigation proceeds, Serpico is advised that his life is in jeopardy from fellow officers, who like the payoff money and fear the consequences. Serpico, while on a raid, is deserted by his partners and is critically wounded, shot in the face.

At the opening of the film we watch his ride to the hospital. Now we hear the doctor report Serpico's progress to his parents. Inspector Sid Green comes to visit Serpico as he is recovering in the hospital and hands him a gold detective's shield, which, out of complete disillusionment, Serpico spitefully rejects. He gives his testimony before the Knapp Commission. Left partially deaf from his wound, he resigns from the police force and, as we watch the titles appear on the screen, moves to "somewhere in Switzerland."

Credits

Producer:	Martin Bregman
Director:	Sidney Lumet
Screenplay:	Waldo Salt and Norman Wexler, based on the book by Peter Maas
Photography:	Arthur J. Ornitz
Art Direction:	Douglas Higgins
Set Decoration:	Thomas H. Wright
Music Composed by:	Mikis Theodorakis
Music Arranged and Conducted by:	Bob James
Sound Editors:	John J. Fitzstephens, Edward Beyer, Robert Reitano and Richard P. Cirincione
Costume Design:	Anna Hill Johnstone
Film Editor:	Dede Allen
Associate Producer:	Roger M. Rothstein
Production Design:	Charles Bailey
Assistant Directors:	Burtt Harris and Alan Hopkins
Make-up:	Redge Tackley

Hair Stylist: Phillip Leto
Wardrobe: Clifford C. Capone
Casting: Shirley Rich
Extra Casting: Talent Services Associated, Inc.
Co-Editor: Richard Marks
Assistant
 Editor: Ronald Roose
Unit Manager: Martin Danzig
Script
 Supervisor: B. J. Bachman
Camera Operator: Louis Barlia
Property Master: Joe Caracciolo
Set Dresser: Les Bloom
Scenic Artist: Jack Hughes
Assistant
 Cameraman: James Hovey
Re-recordist: Richard Vorisek
Sound Mixer: James J. Sabat
Boom-Operator: Robert Rogow
Gaffer: Willy Meyerhoff
Key Grip: Charles Kolb
Production
 Secretary: Shari Leibowitz
Transportation
 Gaffer: Raymond Hartwick
Locations: Cinemobile Systems, Inc.
Publicity: Solters/Sabinson/Roskin
Cast: Al Pacino (Serpico), John Randolph (Sidney Green), Jack Kehoe (Tom Keough), Biff McGuire (Inspector McClain), Barbara Edayoung (Laurie), Cornelia Sharpe (Leslie), Tony Roberts (Bob Blair), John Medici (Pasquale), Allan Rich (D.A. Tauber), Norman Ornellas (Rubello), Ed Grover (Lombardo), Al Henderson (Peluce), Hank Garre (Malone), Damien Leake (Joey), Joe Bova (Potts), Gene Gross (Captain Tolkin), John Stewart (Waterman), Woodie King (Larry), James Tolkin (Steiger), Ed Crowley (Barto), Bernard Barrow (Palmer), Sal Carollo (Mr. Serpico), Mildred Clinton (Mrs. Serpico), Nathan George (Smith), Gus Fleming (Dr. Metz), Richard Foronjy (Corsaro), Alan North (Brown), Lewis J. Stadlen (Berman), John McQuade (Kellogg), Ted Beniades (Sarno), John Lehne (Gilbert), M. Emmet Walsh (Gallagher), George Ede (Daley), Charles White (Delaney).
Filmed on
 location in
 New York
Distribution: Paramount
Running Time: 130 minutes
Color: Technicolor
Equipment: Panavision
Release: February, 1974

Note

For the Academy Awards, Al Pacino was nominated as best actor and Waldo Salt and Norman Wexler were nominated for their screenplay, based on material from another medium.

21 LOVIN' MOLLY (1974)

This film follows the lives of three people from 1925 to 1964. It is narrated by Gid (Perkins), Molly (Danner), and Johnny (Bridges) in turn. They are all farmfolk from Bastrop, Texas.

The film opens on Election Day in 1925 as Gid and his friend Johnny engage in a friendly rivalry for Molly's attention. Molly is a sensuous, free-spirited girl who likes both boys. Because of his conventional attitude, Gid expresses his attraction to Molly by proposing marriage. Molly, also attracted to Gid, wants to share a sexually vital relationship with him, but outside of the restrictions of marriage. She then invites him to go swimming with her in the nude, but Gid, fearing embarrassment, refuses. Gid is also attracted to Sarah (Saranson), with whom he is sexually more open because he is less personal. He tells us, "I wasn't proud of the reasons I went to see Sarah . . . but I went anyway." Molly goes to a dance with Eddie White (Fowkes), another local farmboy, and while there Johnny picks a fight with him. Shortly afterwards, Gid sleeps with Molly and is shocked to discover she is not a virgin. While on the train to the Panhandle to sell Gid's father's cattle, Gid attacks Johnny for sleeping with Molly and not proposing marriage to her. He is further outraged to find that Eddie had slept with her even before Johnny. "I'll marry her anyway," he tells Johnny, "even if I am third man." The cattle are sold. Back home, Gid can neither understand nor accept Molly's attraction to Eddie. Seeking advice from his father, he is told, "A woman's love is like the morning dew: it is just as apt to settle on a horse turd as a rose." Discouraged and restless, he and Johnny leave to find work as cowhands back in the Panhandle. Although Johnny stays on, Gid shortly decides to return home to see Molly. Molly's father has died and she has married Eddie. When Gid's father dies, he inherits the farm and marries Sarah. After some time has passed, Gid and Molly are reunited. While Eddie is away working in the oil fields, Molly reveals her desire to have Gid father her first child.

Now it is 1945, the three are now in middle age, and Molly picks up the narration. Eddie has been killed in an oil rig accident and Molly has two children: Matt, fathered by Gid, and Joe, by Johnny. Joe, who was "so glad" to discover that Johnny was his father, has been killed in the war. Matt is still in the service. Gid has continued to see Molly through the intervening years. Molly receives a letter from Matt revealing that he is ashamed to be Gid's illegitimate son, signing the letter, "your bastard son." Molly, heartbroken, burns this letter and never tells Gid about it. She then receives a notice that Matt has been killed. Gid, hearing the news of his son's death and yielding to social propriety, tells Molly he can no longer continue to see her. "I'm ashamed of us both," Gid tells her. Molly answers him, "All I can say is, if it's wrong than let's you and I have the guts to be wrong. We can't but go to hell for it." Molly continues to see Johnny, who is not troubled by the qualms Gid has. "I never missed a night's sleep from being ashamed," he tells Molly. Gid, in a gesture of reconciliation, brings a puppy for Molly to raise.

Now it is 1964, and they are in old age as Johnny narrates the final chapter. Gid has become a hard-working farmer and land rich. As Johnny's narration opens, Gid is recuperating in the hospital. He and Johnny discuss their relationship with Molly, Gid concerned that it has been immoral and Johnny unconcerned. Johnny talks Gid into leaving the hospital and returning to the farm. At the farm, while repairing a windmill, Gid tells Johnny of his decision "to move in with Molly." Almost as soon as he utters this, he collapses from a stroke. Rejecting Johnny's advice to go to the hospital, Gid tells him, "Take me over to Molly's. Maybe this time I'll have the sense to stay." But Gid dies in Johnny's truck before reaching Molly. After the funeral, Johnny proposes marriage to Molly. She refuses but says she wishes to continue to love him.

Credits

Producer:	Stephen Friedman
Director:	Sidney Lumet
Screenplay:	Stephen Friedman, based on the novel *Leaving Cheyenne* by Larry McMurtry
Photography:	Edward Brown
Art Direction:	Robert Drunheller, Paul Hefferan
Music:	Fred Hellerman
Music Direction:	Samuel Matlovsky
Sound Recordist:	Jack Fitzstephens, John Sabat
Sound Re-recordist:	Sound Shop Inc.
Costumes:	Gene Coffin
Editor:	Joanne Burke
Associate Producer:	David Golden
Production Manager:	John Robert Lloyd
Assistant Director:	Charles Okun
Make-up:	Robert Laden
Production Design:	Gene Coffin
Titles:	F. Hillsberg Inc.
Cast:	Anthony Perkins (Gid), Beau Bridges (Johnny), Blythe Danner (Molly), Edward Binns (Mr. Fry), Susan Saranson (Sarah), Conrad Fowkes (Eddie White), Claude Traverse (Mr. Tayler), John Henry Faulk (Mr. Grinson).
Distribution:	Gala
Running Time:	98 minutes
Color:	Movielab
Release:	March, 1974

22 MURDER ON THE ORIENT EXPRESS (1974)

This film begins with a rapid and fragmentary montage of newspaper accounts from a famous kidnapping case. In 1930, Daisy Armstrong, a small child, had been abducted from her palatial Long Island home. The kidnapping resulted in four deaths: Daisy, her parents and their French maid, who committed suicide because she was under police investigation.

Five years later, at a train station in Istanbul, the Orient Express prepares to leave. An assortment of passengers arrives at the station and boards the train. There are numerous peddlers selling their wares, and deliveries of oysters and meat are being made. The passengers include: Ratchett (Widmark), an unpleasant but wealthy American businessman; Ratchett's secretary (Perkins) and manservant (Gielgud); Princess Dragomiroff (Hiller), a dowager, and her maid (Roberts); Mrs. Hubbard (Bacall), a loquacious American; Greta Ohlsson (Bergman), a missionary from Sweden; Mary Debenham (Redgrave), an English teacher; Count Andrenyi (York), a Hungarian diplomat, and his wife (Bisset); and Colonel Arbuthnot (Connery), a member of the British army. Hercule Poirot (Finney), an internationally famous detective, arrives late and there are no accommodations for him. It is remarked how strange it is that the Orient Express should be filled to capacity at this time of year. Bianchi (Balsam), a director of the railway company and an old friend of Poirot, finally succeeds in finding him a berth at the last minute.

On the first day of the journey, Ratchett approaches Poirot and asks him to be his bodyguard, as Ratchett's life has been threatened. Poirot declines the assignment. The next morning the passengers awake to find the train stalled by a snowslide in Yugoslavia. Ratchett is found dead in his bunk with multiple stab wounds. At Bianchi's request, Poirot announces he will investigate the murder. By piecing together certain scattered clues, Poirot soon discovers that Ratchett was a gangster who had, in fact, masterminded the Daisy Armstrong kidnapping. As Poirot questions each of the passengers, some clues, coincidences and contradictions become apparent. A wagon-lit attendant's uniform and blood-stained dagger are found, suggesting that an unseen murderer had been concealed on the train and escaped. This supports Mrs. Hubbard's claim that she saw an unidentified man pass through her compartment on the night of the killing. After Poirot has finished questioning each passenger, all of whom are suspects, he calls them together to offer two probable solutions to the crime.

He begins his reconstruction by saying, "A repulsive murderer has himself been repulsively, and perhaps deservedly, murdered." The first and most obvious explanation is that another gangster, Ratchett's rival, found out he was on the train, killed him and escaped in the snow. The second explanation, more complex, is that the act was a ritual murder of revenge. By memory and deduction, Poirot has discovered that all eleven of the passengers and Pierre, the wagon-lit attendant, were associated with either the Armstrong family or the disposition of the case. Each, therefore, had a provocation to kill Ratchett. Poirot concludes that together they planned and committed Ratchett's execution, leaving clues to mislead authorities.

Bianchi is told the two stories and asked to choose which one to tell the Yugoslav authorities. Bianchi chooses the first but, in fact, the second story is true.

Credits

Producer:	John Brabourne and Richard Goodwin
Director:	Sidney Lumet
Screenplay:	Paul Dehn, from the novel by Agatha Christie
Photography:	Geoffrey Unsworth, B.S.C.
Art Direction:	Jack Stephens
Production Design and Costumes:	Tony Walton
Music Composed by:	Richard Rodney Bennett
Orchestra of the Royal House, Covent Garden Conducted by:	Marcus Dods
Sound:	Peter Handford, Bill Rowe
Sound Editor:	Jonathan Bates
Wardrobe:	Brenda Dabbs
Editor:	Anne V. Coates
Production Associate:	Richard Du Vivier
Production Manager:	Jack Causey
French Production Manager:	Louis Fleury
First Assistant Director:	Ted Sturgis
Make-up:	Charles Parker, Stuart Freeborn, John O'Gorman
Hairdressing Supervisor:	Ramon Gow
Camera Operator:	Peter MacDonald
Unit Manager:	Jim Brennan
Location Manager:	Norton Knatchbull
Continuity:	Angela Allen
Production Secretary:	Elisabeth Woodthorpe
Process Photography:	Charles Staffell, B.S.C.
Miss Bergman's and Mr. Finney's hair by:	Leonard of London
The Princess's jewellery by:	Wartski

Montage
Sequences
and Titles: Richard Williams' Studios
Cast: Albert Finney (Hercule Poirot), Lauren Bacall (Mrs. Hubbard), Martin Balsam (Bianchi), Ingrid Bergman (Greta Ohlsson), Jacqueline Bisset (Countess Andrenyi), Jean-Pierre Cassel (Pierre Paul Michel), Sean Connery (Colonel Arbuthnot), John Gielgud (Beddoes), Wendy Hiller (Princess Dragomiroff), Anthony Perkins (Hector McQueen), Vanessa Redgrave (Mary Debenham), Rachel Roberts (Hildegarde Schmidt), Richard Widmark (Ratchett), Michael York (Count Andrenyi), Colin Blakely (Hardman), George Coulouris (Doctor Constantine), Der Quilley (Foscarelli), Vernon Dobtcheff (Concierge), Jeremy Lloyd (A.D.C.), John Moffatt (Chief Attendant).
Filmed in Borehamwood, England, and on location in France and Turkey
Distribution: Paramount
Running Time: 128 minutes
Color: Technicolor
Cameras and Lenses: Panavision
Release: December, 1974

Note

Ingrid Bergman won the Academy Award for best supporting actress, while Albert Finney was nominated for best actor; the film also received nominations for best cinematography, best costume design, best dramatic score, and best screenplay adapted from another medium.

23 DOG DAY AFTERNOON (1975)

It is hot on August 22, 1972, in Brooklyn. The opening montage depicts fragments from an ordinary day: street scenes, traffic jams, business signs, water sports. Everyone feels the heat.

Three men walk into a branch of the First Brooklyn Savings Bank and one of them, Sal (Cazale), pulls a gun on the manager, Mulvaney (Boyar). Stevie, the youngest of the three, gets "bad vibes" and tells the leader, Sonny (Pacino), he cannot go through with it. Stevie leaves and Sonny and Sal are left alone with bank personnel. Sonny and Sal hold Mulvaney and his mostly female staff hostage while they proceed with what seems to be a carefully planned robbery. It is obvious that Sonny knows a lot about banks and security systems but soon finds out that he has been misinformed about the money; instead of being delivered, it was picked up earlier in the morning. Taking the $1,100 still left in the bank, Sonny burns the bank records, which would allow authorities to trace the money. The smoke, ventilated out of the building, is seen from the outside. A curious storeowner across the street comes to see if everything is all right; Mulvaney, threatened by Sonny, assures him it is. Soon, Sonny is called by Moretti (Durning), a police officer, who tells Sonny that the bank is surrounded by police. Within moments, a plethora of police units, television crews and sidewalk spectators crowd the street.

Both Sonny and Moretti appear to be at a standoff. Outside, Moretti has difficulty controlling his over-anxious men and the partisan crowd. Trapped inside the bank, Sonny has equal difficulty with his hostages. Howard (Marriott), the security guard, has an asthma attack and must be released. The hostages complain about the breakdown in the air conditioning and one needs to use the bathroom. When Mulvaney, a diabetic, collapses from the lack of insulin, Sonny calls for a doctor. Trying to deal with complaining hostages and an uncomprehending Sal, Sonny bargains with Moretti. After a series of indecisive exchanges, Sonny bargains for an airplane to take him and Sal out of the country. Moretti agrees to Sonny's demand, on condition that he release one hostage for each concession made to him. Moretti advises Sonny that it will take several hours to arrange for the plane. Confident of his position, Sonny tells Sal, "I'm flying to the tropics — fuck the snow. . . . I can make it happen."

An FBI agent, Sheldon (Broderick), has been silently but meticulously observing the whole ordeal. Periodically, Sonny and Moretti have face to face confrontations in the street trying to resolve the situation so that no one gets hurt. Screaming "Attica" to the police, the crowd cheers Sonny ("Sonny all the way!"). The media treats the incident as a sideshow, even interviewing Sonny by telephone while in the bank. In the late afternoon, Sonny demands a visit with his wife. He gives the police the address and they return with Leon (Sarandon), his homosexual wife. Leon, still wearing hospital garments, has just been released from psychiatric care after an attempted suicide, brought on, Leon claims, by Sonny's abusive behavior. Moretti persuades the reluctant Leon to try to convince Sonny to give himself up. He and Sonny speak on the phone, but it only reveals their mutual frustrations. It becomes clear that Sonny staged the whole robbery to finance a sex change operation for Leon. Sonny offers to take Leon with them out of the country but Leon refuses. Sonny's conventional wife, Angie (Peretz), fat and gabby, also speaks to him on the phone, and his mother (Malina) comes to plead with him. Sheldon now takes over the police operation. Offering to make a private deal with Sonny, Sheldon proposes that Sonny betray Sal; Sonny becomes outraged at the idea.

When it is announced that the plane is ready, the hostages form a circle of protection around Sonny and Sal and they begin the trip to the airport in a limousine bus driven by one of Sheldon's agents. Arriving at Kennedy Airport, Sonny believes that he has finally "made it happen." Sheldon suddenly immobilizes Sonny's shotgun; the driver simultaneously kills Sal. The hostages are released as Sonny is cuffed and arrested.

Credits

Producer:	Martin Bregman and Martin Elfand
Director:	Sidney Lumet
Screenplay:	Frank Pierson, based on magazine articles by P. F. Kluge and Thomas Moore
Photography:	Victor J. Kemper
Art Direction:	Doug Higgins
Set Decoration:	Robert Drumheller
Sound Editors:	Jack Fitzstephens, Richard Cirincione, Sanford Rackow and Stephen A. Rotter
Sound Mixer:	James Sabat
Re-recording Supervisor:	Richard Vorasek
Costume Design:	Anna Hill Johnstone
Wardrobe Supervisors:	Cliff Capone, Peggy Farrell
Make-up:	Reginald Tackley
Editor:	Dede Allen
Associate Producer:	Robert Greenhut
Assistant Director:	Burtt Harris
Second Assistant Director:	Alan Hopkins
Script Supervisor:	B. J. Bjorkman
Unit Publicity:	Solters and Roskin
Assistant Editor:	Angelo Corrao
Production Coordinator:	Lois Kramer
Scenic Artist:	Stanley Cappiello
Production Designer:	Charles Bailey
Casting:	Don Phillips and Michael Chinich
Cast:	Al Pacino (Sonny Wortzik), John Cazale (Sal), Penny Allen (Sylvia, the head teller), Sully Boyar (Mulvaney), Beulah Garrick (Margaret), Carol Kane (Jenny), Sandra Kazan (Deborah), Marcia Jean Kurtz (Miriam), Amy Levitt (Maria), John Marriott (Howard), Estelle Omens (Edna), Gary Springer (Bobby), James Broderick (Sheldon), Charles Durning (Moretti), Carmine Foresta (Carmine), Lang Henriksen (Murphy), Floyd Levine (Phone Cop), Thomas Murphy (Policeman with Angie), Dominic Chianese (Sonny's Father), Marcia Haufrecht (Vi's Friend), Judith Malina (Vi, Sonny's Mother), Susan Peretz (Angie), Chris Sarandon (Leon), William Bogert (TV Studio Anchorman), Ron Cummins (TV Reporter), Jay Gerber (Sam), Philip Charles Mackenzie (Doctor), Chu Chu Malave (Maria's Boyfriend), Lionel Pina (Pizza Boy), Dick Williams (Limo Driver).

Filmed on
location in
Brooklyn
Distribution: Columbia-Warner Brothers
Running Time: 130 minutes
Color: Technicolor
Release: October, 1975

Note

The film won an Academy Award for best original screenplay. It also received nominations for best actor (Pacino), best supporting actor (Sarandon), best editor, best director, and best picture.

24 NETWORK (1976)

Howard Beale (Finch), a fifty-eight year old news anchorman at United Broadcasting Systems (UBS), is informed by his friend, Max Shumacher (Holden), the head of the News Division, that he has been fired because his ratings are down. Max and Beale proceed to get drunk, amusing themselves with anecdotes from the past and joking about a "Suicide of the Week" program. Beale shocks everyone by announcing on his next news show that, to protest his dismissal, he will kill himself the following week while on television. After the show and amid all the chaos it has caused, Beale admits his foolishness ("I don't want to go out of life a clown"). Counter to instructions from above, Max allows Beale to do one final farewell show. In the next broadcast, Beale unexpectedly attacks the media, accusing it of bullshit: "Bullshit is all the reasons we give for living." Max is subsequently forced to resign by Edward Ruddy (Prince), the Chairman of the Board, and a replacement for Beale is arranged.

Diana Christenson (Dunaway) is an aggressive Vice-President in charge of programming at UBS. She screens some footage shot by Laureen Hobbs (Warfield) and her Ecumenecal Liberation Army (ELA). The ELA shot the footage at a bank while they were robbing it. Diana feels that this would make a good basis for a weekly series, as the American people, she believes, are angry and need someone to articulate their rage for them. She decides the "Mao Tse Tung Hour" would be an appropriate name and proceeds to negotiate with Laureen Hobbs for subsequent filmed revolutionary events. After seeing the overnight ratings of Howard Beale's news show, Diana convinces Frank Hackett (Duvall), Executive Senior Vice-President of UBS, to put Beale back on the air as "a latter-day prophet denouncing the hypocricies of our time." When Ruddy hears that Hackett has approved this, he, anticipating a power play, asks Max to reconsider his resignation. Max decides to stay on to support Ruddy against Hackett. Beale agrees to do the show. That evening in his office, Diana approaches Max about re-designing Beale's show. Max rejects her proposal to reduce the news to an entertainment format. That night they begin their affair.

Awakened in his sleep the same evening, Beale experiences a mystical revelation. Believing himself to be "imbued with a special spirit," his show — which has changed from news to commentary — takes on an evangelical direction. Max, concerned about his close friend, advises that Beale be removed from the show and placed under psychiatric observation. When Ruddy has a heart attack, control of the network passes to Hackett. Hackett, ruthless but calculating, sees in the Howard Beale phenomenon an opportunity to further his own ambitions of power. Hackett's first act as controller of the network is to take Beale's show from Max's supervision and, in Diana's presence, give it to her. Max is fired and leaves with bitter feelings toward all. Soon "The Howard Beale Show" (Beale is now called "The mad prophet of the air ways") is rated as one of the top four shows on all networks, bringing a much-needed boost to UBS. After Ruddy's funeral, Max and Diana, each reconciled by now, resume their affair. A month later, Max leaves his wife (Straight) of twenty-five years, and moves in with Diana, knowing that it will eventually end in disaster.

One night on his show, Beale attacks the mega-corporations backed by foreign money that are taking over the United States. He is quickly called to see Arthur Jensen (Beatty), an executive of the corporation that owns UBS. Jensen delivers a monologue to Beale on the advantages of a corporate utopia in such a forceful manner that Beale succumbs to his spell. Beale, thinking he has listened to a divine authority, abruptly reverses his advocacies on the program. His discourses on the futility of individual sanctity and collective action result in a sharp and steady decline in ratings. Diana tries to force Beale to change the content of his shows, but Beale insists he says what his voices (Jensen) tell him to. Diana, suffering from compulsive anxiety prompted by her job, drives the more settled Max away from her. Before he leaves, Max condemns the devastating products of both television and the television generation. "You are indifferent to all suffering, insensitive to joy," he tells her. "All of life is reduced to the common rubble of banality . . . you are madness incarnate . . . and whatever you touch dies with you." At a secret meeting later that night, Diana, Hackett and other UBS executives coolly consider what to do about Beale's falling ratings. Since their own positions with UBS are imperilled by Beale's departing audience, the only option they can agree upon is to persuade the ELA to assassinate Beale during his program.

After the televised murder, the off-screen announcer comments, "This was the story of Howard Beale, the first man killed because he had lousy ratings."

Credits

Producer:	Howard Gottfried
Director:	Sidney Lumet
Original story and screenplay:	Paddy Chayefsky
Photography:	Owen Roizman, A.S.C.
Production Design:	Philip Rosenberg

Set Decoration:	Edward Stewart
Original music composed and conducted by:	Elliot Lawrence
Sound Editors:	Jack Fitzstephens, Sanford Rackow, and Marc M. Laub
Re-Recordist:	Dick Vorisek
Sound Mixer:	James Sabat
Costume Design:	Theoni V. Aldredge
Editor:	Alan Heim
Associate Producer:	Fred Caruso
First Assistant Director:	Jay Allan Hopkins
Second Assistant Director:	Ralph Singleton
Make-up:	John Alese
Hair Stylist:	Phil Leto
Casting:	Juliet Taylor/MDA
Camera Operator:	Fred Schuler
Assistant Cameraman:	Tom Priestley, Jr.
Second Assistant Cameraman:	Gary Muller
Assistant Editor:	Michael Jacobi
Still Photographer:	Michael Ginsburg
Key Grip:	Kenneth Goss
Gaffer:	Norman Leigh
Ms. Dunaway's Makeup:	Lee Harman
Ms. Dunaway's Hair:	Susan Germaine
Costumers:	George Newman, Marilyn Putnam
Script Supervisor:	Kay Chapin
Property Master:	Conrad Brink
Location Coordinator:	John Starke
Office Coordinator:	Connie Schoenberg
Production Auditor:	Selma Brown
Extra Casting:	Todd-Champion, Ltd.
UBS video logo:	Steve Rutt, EUE Video Services
Scenic Artist:	Eugene Powell
Television Consultant:	Lynn Klugman
Cast:	Faye Dunaway (Diana Christensen), William Holden (Max Schumacher), Peter Finch (Howard Beale), Robert Duvall (Frank Hackett), Wesley Addy (Nelson Chaney), Ned Beatty (Arthur Jensen), Arthur Burghardt (Great

Ahmed Khan), Bill Burrows (TV Director), John Carpenter (George Bosch), Jordan Charney (Harry Hunter), Kathy Cronkite (Mary Ann Gifford), Ed Crowley (Joe Donnelly), Jerome Dempsey (Walter C. Amundsen), Conchata Ferrell (Barbara Schlesinger), Gene Gross (Milton K. Steinman), Stanley Grover (Jack Snowden), Cindy Grover (Caroline Schumacher), Darry Hickman (Bill Herron), Mitchell Jason (Arthur Zanwill), Paul Jenkins (TV Stage Manager), Ken Kercheval (Merrill Grant), Kenneth Kimmins (Associate Producer), Lynn Klugman (TV Production Assistant), Carolyn Krigbaum (Max's Secretary), Zane Lasky (Audio Man), Michael Lipton (Tommy Pellegrino), Michael Lombard (Willie Stein), Pirie MacDonald (Herb Thackeray), Russ Petranto (TV Associate Director), Bernard Pollock (Lou), Roy Poole (Sam Haywood), William Prince (Edward George Ruddy), Sasha Von Scherler (Helen Miggs), Lane Smith (Robert McDonough), Theodore Sorel (Giannini), Beatrice Straight (Louise Schumacher), Fred Stuthman (Mosaic Figure), Cameron Thomas (TV Technical Director), Marlene Warfield (Laurene Hobbs), Lydia Wilen (Hunter's Secretary), Lee Richardson (Narrator).

Filmed in New York and Toronto
Distribution: United Artists
Running Time: 121 minutes
Color: Metrocolor
Release: December, 1976

Note

Academy Awards were won by Faye Dunaway for best actress, Peter Finch for best actor, Beatrice Straight for best supporting actress, and Paddy Chayefsky for best original screenplay. Nominations were received by William Holden for best actor, Ned Beatty for best supporting actor, Owen Roizman for best cinematography, Alan Heim for best editing, Lumet for best director, and the film for best picture.

25 EQUUS (1977)

The film opens on a daggar with a skull for a handle slowly turning in limbo. As the camera zooms in, we recognize it as the skull of a horse with a bit and harness in place. There is a dissolve to a real horse's head, and we see it is in a field at night, being caressed by a boy. We hear the narrator telling what he feels the horse is thinking, and a slow pan shows us a close up of Martin Dysart (Burton). As the camera zooms out, we see he is sitting at a desk, a scene that will be intercut frequently throughout the film. Dysart tells us that he feels as the horse does, trapped with a bit in his mouth, but decides to explain the whole story; as he begins, the titles appear over several shots of young people in the hospital for mentally troubled children where Dysart works.

As Dysart is in his office, Hester, a concerned lawyer, comes to visit and begs him to take on one more patient, Alan Strang (Firth), who has blinded six horses with a metal spike. Although Dysart does not want to, Hester convinces him he is the only one who can help Alan because he is "extraordinary." We see Alan arriving at the hospital and being shown to his room. Soon, he goes to Dysart's office for his first session. When he asks Alan his age, Alan sings a jingle from a commercial. Alan will not speak but sings a few jingles. He is then taken on a tour of the hospital.

The next scene begins with Dysart behind his desk telling about a nightmare he has had. In the dream, he was some kind of priest. Children lined up in front of him and it was his job to slice the children's stomachs open and take out their organs. At the end of the dream, his mask falls off, the two assistant priests see him and turn to him, and then he wakes up. Intercut with this description are shots of Dysart shaving, dressing, drinking coffee and leaving the house in his car. He goes to the Strang house. Mrs. Strang is a very religious woman. She tells Dysart of Alan's love for horses and takes him to Alan's bedroom to show him the picture of the horse that he treasures. She tells Dysart of the religious training she has given Alan and then Mr. Strang comes home. Discussing horses, the word "Equus" is mentioned — the Latin word for horse. When Mrs. Strang goes for tea, Mr. Strang tells Dysart that she has romantic ideas about her family and is obsessed with religion.

We see a short shot of Alan in his bed calling out "equus" and hitting his thigh with his hand. The next morning Alan walks into Dysart's office to find him still asleep. He slams the door and opens the curtains. Imitating the poses of horses, Alan ignores Dysart's questions. Alan resists answering the questions, so they agree to take turns asking questions. Alan tells of the time he was six years old and playing on the beach. (This sequence, like many others, is in the form of a flashback.) Alan looks up from his sand castle to see a large black horse with a rider. He is in awe. The rider invites him to pet the creature and then takes him for a ride. They trot, canter and then gallop along the water. Alan's parents see and are terribly upset. They order Alan off the horse; when he refuses, he is callously pulled down. Alan tells Dysart he has not ridden a horse since, even when he worked at the stable. Dysart gives Alan a tape recorder to communicate anything he does not feel comfortable saying to Dysart's face. Alan calls it "stupid" but takes it anyway.

That night, we see Dysart at home looking at pictures of horses. Mrs. Strang calls Dysart to tell him there is something she did not tell him about the picture of the horse on Alan's bedroom wall, so the next day Dysart goes to see her. She tells him that Alan used to have a picture of Jesus hanging where the horse is, but Mr. Strang tore it down and got him the horse to replace it. Dysart puts the picture of Jesus next to the horse and we can see how similar they are, both wearing chains. Dysart takes a box of Alan's things with him as he leaves. Dysart goes to visit Mr. Dalton, the man who owns the stable where Alan used to work. Mr. Dalton describes Alan as hard working. Dysart mentions that Alan said he never rode and Mr. Dalton confirms this but says he was suspicious that someone was taking horses out at night. He also says that it was Jill who helped Alan get the job.

Alan is in his room talking into the tape recorder, telling about the time he was at the beach. He says that he asked the horse if the bit hurt and the horse told him that it did. He talks about his obsession with horses and how he must watch them. Dysart goes to talk to Mr. Strang at his printing shop; he tells Dysart an unusual story about Alan. A few months earlier, Mr. Strang was on his way to bed when he heard Alan chanting in his bedroom. Mr. Strang looked in to see him kneeling before the picture of the horse. Alan took a piece of rope and put it in his mouth, as a harness would be put on a horse. In his other hand, he took a wooden hanger and hit himself with it. He also tells Dysart that Alan was out with a girl on the night the horses were blinded. Dysart talks to Alan, who tells him about Jill, how he met her and how he got the job at the stable. Dysart, behind his desk, tells the viewers how vulnerable Alan makes him feel. Dysart goes to see Hester at her home and they talk about how he and his wife are not getting along.

In their next session, Dysart hypnotizes Alan, who then tells about the horse on the beach talking to him, his activities in his bedroom and finally how he used to sneak the horses out at night when he worked at the stable. Every three weeks he would put "sandals" on a horse and take him to a field. Then he would remove his clothes, put a "manbit" in his mouth, have a sort of communion with the horse, using sugar cubes instead of bread, and ride the horse, calling Equus, as a religious experience. Dysart, behind his desk, tells us how he feels displaced and that horses are beginning to upset him. Mrs. Strang comes to visit Alan and they end up in a fight; Dysart asks her to leave and not to come back. Mrs. Strang says, "He was my little Alan and the devil came." Dysart meets with Alan who tells him that everything he has told him about his night rides was a lie. Alan says he knows about the "truth drug." Dysart goes to see Hester and tells her that he is thinking of giving Alan an aspirin and telling him it is a truth drug, although none exists. He confesses to her that he is jealous of Alan. That night he meets with Alan and gives him the "truth drug." Alan tells about the night Jill asked him to take her to a skin flick. Neither of them had been before, so they went. While they were there, Alan's father walked in and dragged Alan out of the theater. They walked to the bus stop, not speaking. Mr. Strang finally told them he was there on business. When the bus came, Alan would not get on. Alan and Jill began the walk home. They arrived at the stable and went to the loft. They took off their clothes and began to make love, but Alan was impotent. All he could see, feel and smell was Equus. He told Jill to leave, and when she did, he felt that Equus was watching. He asked Equus to forgive him. Alan jumped out of the loft, picked up a metal spike and gouged out the eyes of six horses. Mr. Dalton arrived and knocked Alan out. Dysart gives Alan a hypodermic to help him sleep.

Dysart sits behind his desk and tells us that soon Alan will be without pain. Soon, Alan can be with horses and barely remember his past experiences. He says, "... and now for me it never stops — the voice of Equus out of the cave — 'why me, why me, first account for me.'... I stand in the dark with a blade in my hand striking at heads.... there is now in my mouth this sharp chain that never comes out."

Credits

Producer:	Lester Persky and Elliot Kastner
Director:	Sidney Lumet
Screenplay:	Peter Shaffer, from his play
Photography:	Oswald Morris
Art Direction:	Simon Holland
Production Design:	Tony Walton
Music:	Richard Rodney Bennett
Sound Mixer:	Jimmy Sabat
Costume Design:	Tony Walton
Editor:	John Victor-Smith
Associate Producer:	Denis Holt (UK)
Production Supervisor:	Colin Host
First Assistant Director:	David Tringham
Make-up:	Ron Berkley and Ken Brooke
Hairdresser:	James Keeler
Technical Adviser (horses):	Yakima Canutt
Continuity:	Blanche McDermaid
Production Accountant:	Arthur Carroll
Wardrobe Supervision:	Branda Dabbs
Still Photography:	Beverly Rockett
Property Master:	Dave Jordan
Set Dresser:	Gerry Holmes
Special Effects:	Kitt West
Electrical Supervisor:	John Tythe
Construction Manager:	Jack Carter
Production Assistant:	Iris Rose
Casting:	Rose Tobias Shaw and Clare Walker
Cast:	Richard Burton (Dr. Martin Dysart), Peter Firth (Alan Strang), Colin Blakely (Frank Strang), Joan Plowright (Dora Strang), Harry Andrews (Harry Dalton), Eileen Atkins (Magistrate Hester Saloman), Jenny Agutter (Jill Mason), John Wyman (the Horseman), Kate Reid (Margaret Dysart)

Filmed on
  location in
  Toronto and
  England
Distribution: United Artists
Running Time: 137 minutes
Color: Technicolor
Release: November, 1977

Note

Richard Burton was nominated for an Academy Award as best actor, and Peter Firth was nominated as best supporting actor.

Annotated Guide to Writings about Lumet

26 Anon. "Sidney Lumet." *Cinema*, 58 (May 1958), 11.
A brief paragraph in the French film journal about Lumet's career through *Stage Struck*.

27 Moskowitz, Gene. "The Tight Close-Up." *Sight and Sound*, 28, Nos. 3-4 (Summer-Autumn 1959), 126-130.
Mr. Moskowitz discusses the changes that have taken place in American television. It used to be, he argues, that the television writer was not given much respect, but now he is highly respected and paid. It was difficult for writers to write creatively when they had to think about commercial interruptions and leave the show on an "upbeat" so that viewers would stay tuned. Television was also very financially restricted. By 1954, however, television was given more prestige, and therefore more money could be invested in production. Television began to comment on important issues and take a firmer stand on morality, while the cinema was veering the other way. Television is hampered by sponsors dictating content and treatment; Moskowitz provides several pertinent examples of sponsor influence on scripts. Attitudes of television, cinema and theatre mutually affect one another.
Many television directors have abandoned television since live production ceased. Some are now in the cinema or theatre, or both. Three such directors are discussed: John Frankenheimer, Robert Mulligan and Sidney Lumet. Lumet explains that he can only work in a "white heat," that his inspiration is the energy generated by continuous work. This, he suggests, comes from his television training. He does not, and will not, work in Hollywood. His *Stage Struck* was a tribute to the theatre. *That Kind of Woman* lost some of its simplicity after it was sent to Hollywood to be scored and re-cut. He states that the closeup is important but should be used wisely. He also mentions the possibilities of magnetic tape.

28 Foster, Frederick. "Filming *The Fugitive Kind.*" *American Cinematographer*, 41, No. 6 (June 1960), 354-355, 379-380, 382.
This article concerns Boris Kaufman's cinematography on the film. It is especially valuable for the comments about Kaufman's working relationship with Lumet.

29 Anon. "Personality of the Month: Sidney Lumet." *Films and Filming*, 6,

No. 11 (August 1960), 5.
A capsule notice about Lumet, suggesting promise for his filming of *The Fugitive Kind*.

30 Bogdanovich, Peter. "An Interview with Sidney Lumet." *Film Quarterly*, 14, No. 2 (Winter 1960), 18-23.
In this extended interview, Lumet discusses many things, starting with his most recent film (*The Fugitive Kind*). He goes on to stress the differences between television and film directing, arguing that, since the television screen is much smaller, the director must know how to focus attention more precisely. He does not feel that films should be shown on television since they were intended for a much larger screen. Lumet also talks about the differences between film directing and stage directing, complaining about the restrictive financial set-up in filmmaking. Lumet admits that he is not, and does not try to be, a writer.
Lumet explains his dislike for Hollywood, claiming that it "has no reason for being." He does not believe that independents have raised the level of films, and he suggests that actors dominate the market. Lumet thinks wide screen, CinemaScope and stereophonic sound are "ridiculous" but concedes that there is no choice, that many directors are forced into shooting with these devices whether they want to or not. Since films are shot out of sequence, Lumet feels there is a big problem for actors because they cannot concentrate on the development of their roles. The subject of critics is brought up, and Lumet suggests that many bits of praise as well as attacks are caused by accidents in filmmaking. Finally, Lumet expresses his wish to work in television, film and theatre, without giving up any.

31 Anon. "Why Am I Happy?" *Newsweek*, 57, No. 24 (12 June 1961), 94.
This brief but thoughtful description-interview of Lumet while making *A View from the Bridge* discusses several important aspects of Lumet's ideas on film. One such topic concerns Lumet's suspicion of the happy ending. "I am strangely interested in unhappy endings," he relates.

32 A. F. "Lumet, Sidney." *Film Ideal*, No. 107 (11 January 1962), p. 626.
A brief bio-filmography.

33 Hirshfield, Gerald. "Low Key for *Fail Safe*." *American Cinematographer*, 44, No. 8 (August 1963), 462-463, 482-484.
An article on photographing the film, written by the cinematographer.

34 Bean, Robin. "The Insider: Sidney Lumet Talks to Robin Bean about His Work in Films." *Films and Filming*, 11, No. 9 (June 1965), 9-13.
This article begins by explaining the relationship between television and film, pointing out that studios are beginning to expand to make films for television. Because of the rapid development, the quality of these television films is poor. In the years of live television, directors had to be quite talented in handling actors, camera work and editing. They had to be able to make many split-second decisions. Three talented young television directors migrated from television to film when pre-filmed shows began to replace live ones: Franklin Schaffner, John Frankenheimer and Sidney Lumet. All three have made progressive steps with each film they have completed, and they know how to involve the audience.
This article deals mainly with the work and progress of Lumet. He has been the

most erratic of the three. There is a short biography of Lumet through his television years. Lumet feels there were two technical contributions that he learned from his television experience: first, the emotional meaning of lenses, and, second, the process of editing. He feels he mastered editing so well in television that, despite the challenge of the three hundred and eighty-five set-ups in *Twelve Angry Men*, there was not one technical error.

The remainder of the article summarizes, critiques and compares *Stage Struck, That Kind of Woman, Long Day's Journey into Night, The Fugitive Kind, A View from the Bridge, Fail Safe, The Group, The Pawnbroker,* and *The Hill*. The author points out that *Stage Struck* was "enchanting" except for Susan Strasberg's performance. Sophia Loren gave her best American film performance in *That Kind of Woman*, and the film as a whole was "well controlled." (Lumet comments that it is harder to work on the smaller television screen than the larger film screen.) Lumet relates that he made *Stage Struck* and *That Kind of Woman* simply because he could work in New York, which is important to him. There is a detailed analysis of Tennessee Williams and *Long Day's Nourney into Night*. Lumet chose *Fail Safe* because the book was so popular, and he felt the anti-war theme had much value at the time.

35 Casty, Alan. "*The Pawnbroker* and the New Direction in Film Realism." *Film Heritage*, 1, No. 3 (Spring 1966), 3-14.

Mr. Casty begins by praising *The Pawnbroker*, claiming it is "a new direction in American film realism." He goes on to explain the traditional realist film, mentioning surface realism and a "true to life" style. He argues that when a more serious film was wanted, social or political problems were added; but the problems all had clear-cut solutions. He explains the settings of these films, saying they are similar to the gangster films of the thirties. (It seems that European films have broken this tradition.) Elia Kazan's *On the Waterfront* is a good example of the changing trend; Robert Rossen's *The Hustler* is also mentioned.

Mr. Casty then examines *The Pawnbroker*. It is, he argues, "a film about the emotional life of man." The main element in the film is the paralleling of past and present, through the use of flashbacks. This process is described in much detail, as is the plot. Some of the visual effects, Mr. Casty claims, are not successful, and he explains them. Then he goes on to mention *Twelve Angry Men, Stage Struck, The Fugitive Kind, Long Day's Journey into Night* and *Fail Safe*. He claims that, in all of Lumet's better films, "we can trace this common element of a gradual revelation of the truth of character and situation, and a final facing up to the meaning of this truth."

36 Steele, Robert. "Another Trip to the Pawnshop." *Film Heritage*, 1, No. 3 (Spring 1966), 15-22.

Robert Steele contributes criticism to two monthly publications. He states that he selects which films he writes about and decided to discuss *The Pawnbroker* after it had received so much praise. After seeing it a second time, he still maintains that it is a failure. Mr. Steele then proceeds through an extended and detailed analysis of various elements which he contends blemish the film. The only positive things said about *The Pawnbroker* concern Lumet's choice of locations and his technical skills.

37 Grönstedt, Olle, Bo Johan Hultman and Torsten Manns. "Samtal om Pantlanaren." *Chaplin*, No. 64 (May 1966), pp. 176-177.

A discussion of Lumet's career and his films, especially *The Pawnbroker*.

38 Young, Freddie. "A Method of Pre-Exposing Color Negative for Subtle Effect." *American Cinematographer*, 47, No. 8 (August 1966), 536-537.

An article by the cinematographer of *The Deadly Affair*, in which he describes how he and Lumet evolved and used the process of pre-exposing the film stock for *The Deadly Affair*.

39 Anon. "Sidney Lumet." *Current Biography*, 28 (September 1967), 258-260.

A non-interpretative survey of Lumet's career, from childhood through *Bye, Bye Braverman*.

40 Petrie, Graham. "The Films of Sidney Lumet: Adaptation as Art." *Film Quarterly*, 21, No. 2 (Winter 1967-1968), 9-18.

Some say, "Lumet is an intelligent, sensitive interpreter of other people's work, who is most successful when he keeps himself in the background and confines himself to unobtrusive direction of actors and creation of atmosphere." Mr. Petrie devotes his article to disproving this. He begins by citing *Twelve Angry Men*, *Long Day's Journey into Night*, *A View from the Bridge* and *The Fugitive Kind* as examples of Lumet's technical excellence. These films are elaborated on and compared as films made from plays. Next, the films from novels are discussed. *Fail Safe* is compared to *Dr. Strangelove*. *The Pawnbroker's* plot and style are discussed at length. The difference between the novel and film versions of *The Group* are mentioned. *The Deadly Affair* is Lumet's most recent film (at the time of the article); the plot is examined and explained. Lumet is in a better position than most directors, Petrie concludes, because he chooses what to work on, works mostly in New York and England, and has cooperative and sympathetic producers.

41 Kael, Pauline. "The Making of *The Group*," in *Kiss Kiss Bang Bang*. New York: Atlantic Monthly Press, 1968, pp. 65-100.

Ms. Kael was invited to observe the entire production of *The Group* — from casting to rehearsals to shooting to editing to preview. This is an important piece, even though Ms. Kael comes down hard on Lumet as a representative of television-trained directors.

Sidney Buchman adapted Mary McCarthy's novel; Sidney Lumet was chosen to direct, because he was "cheap, fast, and reliable." Lumet works fast and will not ask for extra days to get a particular scene just how he wants it. "From what I observed, Lumet's planning is based on the hope that he'll come out of the shooting with something he can pull together in the editing room." He is doing a job and is rather mechanical about it; he is satisfied to be a one-dimensional director. Both Lumet and Buchman seemed more concerned with what they would be doing after *The Group* than with the present project.

During rehearsals, Lumet would tell the actresses of his own experiences so that they could better understand what the Depression was like; he did not talk about the screenplay or its interpretation. He is a "method director": ". . . he looked for the meaning and motivation of everything in himself and his own experience. . . ." Ms. Kael faults much of the film for not being faithful to the novel and faults Lumet for his apparent insensitivity to it. Lumet has trouble with camera movement and background space, which is typical of television-trained directors.

When Lumet mentioned some of his ambitious plans to Ms. Kael, she responded by telling him that he could not handle it. He replied, "I can learn. I just have to give it some time." Lumet works best under pressure and if it is not there, he creates it. "[H]e operates on a wing and a prayer. . . . For sheer guts, Lumet is awe-inspiring."

42 Kerner, Bruce. "An Interview with Kenneth Hyman." *Cinema* (Beverly Hills), 4, No. 2 (Summer 1968), 5-9.
Kenneth Hyman produced *The Hill*. This interview deals mostly with the film, although much of it provides insight on Lumet. Mr. Hyman first saw *The Hill* as a play, convinced Seven Arts to buy the playscript and asked Lumet to direct it. They went to Almeria, Spain, with Ozzie Morris, the cinematographer, and a few others to test footage. Lumet rehearsed with the actors, antagonizing and baiting them. When the film was completed, Hyman had so much faith in Lumet that he made a contract with him that gives Lumet complete autonomy with any film he does for Hyman.

43 Anon. "Midtersiderne: 107 Hollywood Instruktorer. Et Leksikon af Per Calum og Morten Piil." *Kosmorama*, No. 87 (1968), p. xiii.
A brief bio-filmography.

44 Cowie, Peter. "Five Directors of the Year," in *International Film Guide*. Vol. 5. Edited by Peter Cowie. London: Tantivy Press, 1968, pp. 20-25.
Lumet was selected as one of the *International Film Guide's* top five directors for 1968 (along with Michelangelo Antonioni, Joris Ivens, Jan Nemec and Bo Widerberg). This is a brief survey and filmography of Lumet's career through *Bye, Bye Braverman*. See no. 54 for a more complete annotation.

45 Sarris, Andrew. *The American Cinema: Directors and Directions, 1929-1968*. New York: E. P. Dutton, 1968, 197-198.
A brief but important critical assessment by the noted *auteur* critic. Sarris takes Lumet's career through *The Appointment*. In general, Sarris does not believe that Lumet will ever rise above "the middle-brow aspirations of his projects." He suggests that, at least in part, the reason for this is Lumet's failure to dominate the films he directs. Sarris places Lumet in the seventh echelon (of eleven), called "Strained Seriousness."

46 Labarca, Daniel. "Sidney Lumet y Su Obra." *Cine al dia*, No. 7 (March 1969), pp. 28-29.
A survey of Lumet's films through *The Deadly Affair*.

47 Farber, Stephen. "Lumet in '69." *Sight and Sound*, 38, No. 4 (Autumn 1969), 190-195.
This article examines Lumet's style and then analyzes several of his films. Lumet is known as an ambitious director "with an eye for the 'prestige' picture, the socially conscious theme, and the flashy, pretentious trick of composition and cutting." He is known to work well with actors, but many feel he is clumsy and an imitator. After making *The Hill* and *The Pawnbroker*, the style and mood of *The Group* was quite different. In these films, as well as *The Deadly Affair, Bye, Bye Braverman* and *The Sea Gull*, Lumet experimented with subject matter and style. He has refined his style, according to Farber.

Lumet does not write his scripts and selects only those that interest him. He usually chooses material from established writers, such as Tennessee Williams and Eugene O'Neill. The flashbacks in *The Pawnbroker* and the opening scene of *The Group* are discussed. The beginning scene of *Bye, Bye Braverman* is suggested as similar to the corresponding scene in *The Group*. *The Sea Gull* is also analyzed. There is an expansive explanation of *The Appointment*. Finally, Farber comments on Lumet's willingness and daring to attempt many things. He has been accused of copying others, but Farber contends that this is not wrong if it is appropriate.

48   Luciano, Dale. "*Long Day's Journey into Night*: An Interview with Sidney Lumet." *Film Quarterly*, 25, No. 1 (Fall 1971), 20-29.

This interview with Lumet provides much information about the making of *Long Day's Journey into Night*. Lumet was dissatisfied with the stage version, so his film differs in significant ways. It was difficult to film, using just four characters and one set. Lumet discusses his technical problems and solutions; in particular, he comments on lighting techniques and lens selections, both of which, he feels, were crucial elements in the film. He also describes the four actors and how each of them worked with their roles. Rehearsals were held and the shooting time was very short. He feels that if the shooting time had been longer, not everyone would have been able to hold up. Lumet worked closely with the editor, although he did not have final cut rights.

49   Merrill, Susan. "Sidney Lumet: *The Offence*. An Interview with Susan Merrill." *Films in Review*, 24, No. 9 (November 1973), 523-528, 556.

Ms. Merrill interviewed Lumet, at his home, about his process and style of direction. (The interview took place shortly before the filming of *The Offence*.) Lumet uses scripts that interest him but does not write; he feels that scriptwriting is a totally different talent than directing. Lumet uses many close-ups. Lumet often chooses actors because he "feels" they fit the script. He is known to get along well with actors; he feels this is because he is "genuinely interested in them." Lumet holds extensive rehearsals with his actors but is quick with the shooting. He believes this is because of his television training.

He had felt hostile to color because it was not being used well; he has since altered his opinion. Lumet chooses scripts that show a conflict in a character's past-and-present situation. Lumet will not, however, discuss the meaning of his films, because "I think there is too much articulation about the meaning of movies today." Lumet concludes by discussing new scriptwriters. He feels that there are exciting opportunities for scriptwriters now, since the collapse of Hollywood production has opened the way for a new seriousness and expression in writing.

50   Anon. "Lumet, Sidney." *Filmlexicon degli autori e delle opere: Aggiormente e Integrazioni, 1958-1971.* Vol 3. Edited by Aldo Bernardini. Rome: Edizioni di Bianco e Nero, 1973, p. 1151.

A brief entry about Lumet that covers his early career and films through *Stage Struck*.

51   Flatley, Guy. "Lumet — the Kid Actor Who Became a Director." *The New York Times* (20 January 1974), sec. 2, pp. 11, 13.

A survey-interview done after the release of *Serpico*, in which Lumet comments on his career and films.

52 Sharples, Win, Jr. "The Filming of *Serpico*." *Filmmakers Newsletter*, 7, No. 4 (February 1974), 30-34.
A description of the problems and solutions in making *Serpico*.

53 Gow, Gordon. "What's Real? What's True?" *Films and Filming*, 21, No. 8 (May 1975), 10-16.
This article discusses several of Lumet's films starting with *Dog Day Afternoon*. The film was based on fact, as was *Serpico*. *Murder on the Orient Express* differs from the other films he has directed. Lumet is dissatisfied with *Bye, Bye Braverman* and feels he could have done much better had he exerted more control. He feels the same about *The Group*.
After a short biography, Lumet's technique in filming *Twelve Angry Men* are discussed. Lumet says, "I'm never really concerned about the originality of something. All I think about is whether it's necessary." Bow quotes Lumet on the problems of filming *The Fugitive Kind*, especially working with Brando and Magnani. Lumet wanted to do *Stage Struck* because of his love for the theatre; but he feels he could have done better. As for *That Kind of Woman*, Lumet feels it was "pretty crummy" but contends that he still likes the first forty-five minutes. Lumet also comments on *Long Day's Journey into Night* and *Fail Safe*. He claims he was surprised at the success of *The Pawnbroker*, as it was his first "really big grosser." *The Hill* is discussed, as is the murder scene in *The Deadly Affair*. *Blood Kin* (*Last of the Mobile Hot-Shots* in the United States), *The Anderson Tapes*, *The Offence* and *Serpico* are also briefly mentioned.

54 Cowie, Peter. *50 Major Film-Makers*. London: Tantivy Press, 1975, pp. 160-164.
This is an expanded survey of Cowie's early assessment of Lumet's career in the *International Film Guide*. The article begins with a brief biography of Lumet. Cowie tersely discusses Lumet's films through *Dog Day Afternoon*, pointing out his passion for theatre and love of dialogue. The most tragic thing that happens to many of Lumet's characters is their loss of faith and feeling, most evident in such films as *The Pawnbroker* and *The Hill*. Another typical Lumet character is one who rebels against those who cannot interpret regulations sanely. Cowie argues that recently Lumet's career "has lost some of its personal ring," mentioning *Bye, Bye Braverman, The Appointment* and *The Sea Gull*. *Serpico* seemed to be the most "likable" of his recent endeavors. Finally, it is observed that although *Murder on the Orient Express* was a box-office success, Lumet has much more to give us.

55 Roizman, Owen. "*Network*, And How It Was Photographed." *American Cinematographer*, 58, No. 4 (April 1977), 384-385, 392.

56 H. H. "Sidney Lumet." *Skoop*, No. 5 (June-July 1977), pp. 12-13, 22.
A cursory survey and filmography of Lumet's work through *Network*.

List of Performances and Writings (and Other Film-related Activities)

STAGE PERFORMANCES

1935

57 *The Brownsville Grandfather* by Abraham Blum; as "an alert and warm-hearted youngster." (The Folks Theatre, New York)

58 *Dead End* by Sidney Kingsley; as one of "Three Small Boys." (The Belasco Theatre, New York)

1936

59 *It Can't Happen Here* adapted by John C. Moffitt and Sinclair Lewis, from the novel by Lewis; Lumet appeared in an unidentified role in the Yiddish version of the Broadway play, presented by the Federal Theatre Project, translated by Benjamin Ressler and Benson Inge. (The Adelphi Theatre, New York)

1937

60 *The Eternal Road* by Franz Werfel, translated by Ludwig Lewisohn and adapted by William A. Drake; as "The Estranged One's Son." (Manhattan Opera House, New York)

1938

61 *Sunup to Sundown* by Francis Edwards Faragoh; as Stanley. (Hudson Theatre, New York)

62 *Schoolhouse on the Lot* by Joseph A. Fields and Jerome Chodorov; as Mickey. (Ritz Theatre, New York)

1939

63 *My Heart's in the Highlands* by William Saroyan; as Johnny. (New York)

64 *Christmas Eve* by Gustav Eckstein; as Leo McGlory. (Henry Miller's Theatre, New York)

1940

65 *Morning Star* by Sylvia Regan; as Hymie Tashman. (Longacre Theatre, New York)

66 *Journey to Jerusalem* by Maxwell Anderson; as the young Jesus. (The National Theatre, New York)

1941

67 *Brooklyn, U. S. A.* by John Bright and Asa Bordages; as Willie Berg. (Forrest Theatre, New York)

1946

68 *A Flag Is Born* by Ben Hecht; as David (Lumet replaced Marlon Brando in the original cast). (Alvin Theater, New York)

1948

69 *Seeds in the Wind* by Arthur Goodman; as Tonya. (Empire Theater, New York)

FILM PERFORMANCES

1939

70 *One Third of a Nation* as Joey Rogers. d: Dudley Murphy

1940

71 *Journey to Jerusalem* as the youthful Jesus. d: Nu Art for Theatre-on-Film, Inc.

TELEVISION DIRECTING

As of this writing, there is no available source (including Lumet himself) that lists credits for television directors. Larry Gianakos' forthcoming book, *Television Drama Series Programming: A Comprehensive Chronicle, 1959-1975* (Scarecrow Press) might prove helpful.

STAGE DIRECTING

1949

72 *The Bourgeois Gentleman* by Moliere. (Cherry Lane Theatre [off-Broadway], New York)

1955

73 *The Doctor's Dilemma* by George Bernard Shaw. (Phoenix Theatre, New York)

1956

74 *Night of the Auk* by Arch Oboler. (The Playhouse, New York)

1960

75 *Caligula* by Albert Camus, adapted by Justin O'Brien. (54th Street Theatre, New York)

1962

76 *Nowhere To Go But Up* by James Lipton (lyrics) and Sol Berkowitz (music). (Winter Garden Theatre, New York)

WRITINGS

77 Lumet, Sidney. "Le Point de Vue du Metteur en Scene." *Cahiers du Cinema*, No. 94 (April 1959), pp. 32-34.

This is an article by Lumet translated into the French by Louis Marcorelles. Largely drawing examples from one of his *Danger* episodes, "The Paper-Box Kid", Lumet discusses his philosophy of directing and method of working. He asserts that a director's function is to give the production a unity. Rather than impinging upon the actors, writers, photographers, designers, he views his function as uniting these disparate contributions into an organic whole. Lumet suggests that the director has four phases in preparing a show: (1) discovering the appropriate "point of view" (that is, not the plot but the best approach to the material) for the work; (2) securing a coherence in casting between the players and their roles; (3) solving problems of set design to reveal both the theme and characters; (4) when rehearsals begin, working out the staging and camera positions.

78 Lumet, Sidney. "On a Film 'Journey.'" *The New York Times* (7 October 1962), sec. 2, p. 7.

Lumet wrote this article on his film *Long Day's Journey into Night*. He mentions that there was no screenwriter and that the script was O'Neill's full text, with only eleven pages cut. Lumet defends the length of the play, claiming that it is needed to express the human experiences involved. He particularly explicates the character of Mary Tyrone and her addiction to narcotics. Lumet explains how the film is different from a photographed stage play in that a fifth character is added to the film version (i.e., the camera). Lumet feels that as much or more can be expressed in silent shots of the human face as "a chariot race." He adds that neither silence nor dialogue is right or wrong; they are just different conceptual thoughts. Lumet hopes that audiences will get more out of the film than they could from the play.

79 Lumet, Sidney. "Sidney Lumet." *Cahiers du Cinema*, Nos. 150-151 (December 1963/January 1964), pp. 56-57.

This piece prints Lumet's responses to six questions concerning the status of filmmaking in the United States. Lumet comments that the way the American film industry finances and distributes movies tends to lower the quality of filmmaking by attempting to satisfy everyone's tastes. It's the fear of financial ruin, he suggests, that prompts the current race by filmmakers towards security, caution and safety in film production — all of which contribute to eroding standards in

American films. Lumet further indicates that he wants to do something original (personal ideas and expressions), but the nature of financing films precludes this possibility. Filmmaking is better in New York than Hollywood, but even so Lumet foresees the trend becoming increasingly more oppressive. He concludes: "I know most of these answers appear pessimistic. Curiously, I have been able to do my own work with considerable freedom from the restraints I'm complaining about here. But I've only been able to do it by keeping away from Hollywood."

80   Lumet, Sidney. "Keep Them on the Hook." *Films and Filming*, 11, No. 1 (October 1964), 17-20.
In this article, Lumet discusses his ideas about *The Pawnbroker*. Lumet reveals that the entire idea behind the film is that no matter "how brutal life is, one must go on." He is pleased that the protagonist (Nazerman) is so unconventional: "the man is an absolute bastard." Lumet deliberately structured the film to be unsentimental. Nazerman, he claims, wants to be with people he can dislike because he is not strong enough to hate anyone. Lumet also comments on Edward Lewis Wallant, the author of the novel, and gives a brief explication of the story. Lumet tells how he began working on the film only two weeks before it was scheduled to be shot and then had to cast everyone (except Rod Steiger) and scout locations. Lumet relates how he decided to use the quick "shock cuts" to depict Nazerman's past. Finally, he suggests that this same cutting technique, which was regarded as avant garde in the film, had been used in television much earlier.

81   Lumet, Sidney. "Why I Like It Here: A Statement by Sidney Lumet." *Making Films in New York*, 1, No. 1 (March 1969), 17.
In this brief article, Lumet explains why he prefers to make films in New York. Making films is a team effort, emotionally and physically strenuous for everyone involved. Although he points out some of the frustrating difficulties of filmmaking, he argues that filmmaking in New York is a more personal experience. "It's this spirit of working together with a no-nonsense crew that epitomizes filming in New York for me," he concludes.

82   Lumet, Sidney. "Sidney Lumet on The Director," in *Movie People: At Work in the Business of Film*. Edited by Fred Baker, with Ross Firestone. New York: Douglas Book Corporation, 1972, pp. 35-50.
This article is in two parts. The first part, written in 1968, describes Lumet's feelings about filmmaking, money and directors. The second part, written in 1970, is an updated version of his earlier statement.
Lumet begins by reducing filmmaking to its simplest terms: "Everything that happens to a film . . . comes down to one very simple thing — money." He illustrates the enormous sums of money needed to shoot and release a film by sharing a financial break-down he had made for one of his films. He discusses the distribution fees, advertising expenses, as well as such costly items as freight, taxes, checking, etc. He points out that once the film is shot, that is hardly the end of the director's problems. He complains that someone else, who often has no understanding of the rationale, makes the final cut on his films. Lumet claims that one cannot wait for circumstances to suit him but must push ahead and "do it."
In 1970, reviewing his earlier thoughts, Lumet still feels that money is most important — and now so tight in the industry that companies have no option but to make low-budget films. Loans are hard to get, and only a few directors have

final cut rights. He discusses screenwriting and improvisation and feels that directors do not need to be writers. Since he has been an actor himself, Lumet feels he can relate well to actors. Since filmmaking is a collaborative effort, he relishes the notion that "the magic *is* in the *community* of it." Lumet feels that every director reveals something of himself in each film.

Reviews and References

83 TWELVE ANGRY MEN
Film Culture, 3 (1957), 14-15.
Monthly Film Bulletin, 24 (1957), 67-68.
Film Daily (27 February 1957), p. 6.
Variety (27 February 1957).
Motion Picture Herald (2 March 1957), p. 281.
Hollywood Reporter (28 March 1957), p. 3.
New York Times Magazine (31 March 1957), pp. 64-65.
National Parent Teacher, 51 (April 1957), 39.
New York Times (7 April 1957), II, p. 5.
Library Journal, 82 (15 April 1957), 1047.
Newsweek, 49 (15 April 1957), 113.
New York Times (15 April 1957), p. 24.
Today's Cinema (18 April 1957), p. 7.
Commonweal, 66 (19 April 1957), 65.
Saturday Review, 40 (20 April 1957), 29.
New York Times (21 April 1957), II, p. 1.
Kinematograph Weekly (25 April 1957), p. 17.
America, 97 (27 April 1957), 150+.
Nation, 184 (27 April 1957), 379.
New Yorker, 33 (27 April 1957), 664.
Time, 69 (29 April 1957), 94+.
Films in Review, VIII (May 1957), 221-222.
Films and Filming, 3 (June 1957), 23.
Telecine, 69 (October 1957).
Cahiers du Cinema, 77 (December 1957), 57.
Positif, 27 (February 1958), 45.
Revue Internationale del Cine (March 1958), p. 58.

84 STAGE STRUCK
New York Times (10 February 1957), p. 5.
Filmfacts, 1 (1958), 62.
Monthly Film Bulletin, No. 293 (1958), p. 73.

Hollywood Reporter (26 February 1958), p. 3.
Variety (26 February 1958).
Films in Review, IX (March 1958), 142-143.
Motion Picture Herald (1 March 1958), p. 732.
Film Daily (6 March 1958), p. 6.
Saturday Review, 41 (22 March 1958), 41.
Time, 71 (7 April 1958), 83-84+.
Library Journal, 83 (15 April 1958), 1180+.
New York Times (23 April 1958), p. 40.
America, 99 (3 May 1958), 180.
New Yorker, 34 (3 May 1958), 62.
New York Times (11 May 1958), II, p. 1.
New Republic, 138 (12 May 1958), 21-22.
Daily Cinema (14 May 1958), p. 4.
Kinematograph Weekly (15 May 1958), p. 13.
Sight and Sound, 27 (Summer 1958), 253.
Films and Filming, 4 (July 1958), 26-27.
Bianco e Nero (January 1959), p. 63.

85   THAT KIND OF WOMAN
Filmfacts, II (1959), 213+.
Filmkritik, No. 8 (1959), p. 224.
Monthly Film Bulletin, No. 311 (1959), p. 156.
New York Times (20 July 1959), II, p. 5.
Film Daily (10 August 1959), p. 6.
Hollywood Reporter (10 August 1959), p. 3.
Variety (12 August 1959).
Motion Picture Herald (15 August 1959), p. 372.
Saturday Review, 42 (5 September 1959), 31.
Newsweek, 54 (7 September 1959), 79.
New York Times (12 September 1959), p. 12.
Daily Cinema (16 September 1959), p. 9.
New Yorker, 35 (19 September 1959), 89+.
Time, 74 (21 September 1959), 107.
Kinematograph Weekly (24 September 1959), p. 10.
Coronet, 46 (October 1959), 10.
Films and Filming, 6 (November 1959), 24.
Sight and Sound, 29 (Winter 1959-1960), 40.

86   THE FUGITIVE KIND
New York Times (5 July 1959), II, p. 5.
New York Times (8 December 1959), p. 58.

Filmkritik, No. 12 (1960), p. 360.
Monthly Film Bulletin, No. 318 (1960), p. 90.
Film Daily (13 April 1960), p. 6.
Hollywood Reporter (13 April 1960), p. 3.
Variety (13 April 1960), p. 6.
New York Times (15 April 1960), p. 13.
Motion Picture Herald (16 April 1960), p. 660.
Time, 75 (18 April 1960), 81.
New Yorker, 36 (23 April 1960), 147.
Saturday Review, 43 (23 April 1960), 28.
New York Times (24 April 1960), II, p. 1.
Newsweek, 55 (25 April 1960), 115.
Commonweal, 72 (29 April 1960), 127.
Films in Review, XI (May 1960), 290-292.
New Republic, 142 (2 May 1960), 21-22.
American Cinematographer, 41 (June 1960), 354-355+.
Film Quarterly, XIII (Summer 1960), 47-49.
Sight and Sound, 29 (Summer 1960), 144-145.
Kinematograph Weekly (1 September 1960), p. 20.

87 VIEW FROM THE BRIDGE
New York Times (16 April 1961), II, p. 7.
Variety (18 October 1961).
Filmkritik, No. 2 (1962), p. 81.
Monthly Film Bulletin, No. 338 (1962), p. 37.
Time, 79 (19 January 1962), 55.
New York Times (21 January 1962), II, p. 9.
Newsweek, 59 (22 January 1962), 80-81.
Hollywood Reporter (23 January 1962), p. 3.
New York Times (23 January 1962), p. 36.
Film Daily (25 January 1962), p. 6.
New Yorker, 37 (27 January 1962), 82.
New York Times (28 January 1962), II, p. 1.
Motion Picture Herald (31 January 1962), p. 427.
Esquire, 57 (February 1962), 22+.
Films in Review, XIII (February 1962), 102-103.
Daily Cinema (5 February 1962), p. 6.
Kinematograph Weekly (8 February 1962), p. 9.
Commonweal, 75 (9 February 1962), 518.
Nation, 194 (10 February 1962), 125.
New Republic, 146 (12 February 1962), 26-27.
Films and Filming, 8 (April 1962), 29.

Sight and Sound, 31 (Spring 1962), 95-96.
Film, No. 32 (Summer 1962), pp. 17-18.
Film Quarterly (Summer 1962), p. 27.

88 LONG DAY'S JOURNEY INTO NIGHT
Motion Picture Herald (22 November 1961), p. 5.
Cinema, 1 (1962), 33.
Cinematique Francais (26 May 1962), p. 8.
Variety (30 May 1962).
Sight and Sound (Summer 1962), p. 131.
Film, No. 33 (Autumn 1962), p. 21.
New Republic, 147 (24 September 1962), 26+.
Films in Review, XIII (October 1962), 486-488.
Theatre Arts, 46 (October 1962), 16-18+.
Saturday Review, 45 (6 October 1962), 30.
New York Times (7 October 1962), II, p. 7.
Hollywood Reporter (10 October 1962), p. 3.
New York Times (10 October 1962), p. 57.
Time, 80 (12 October 1962), 102+.
Nation, 195 (13 October 1962), 227-228.
New York Times (14 October 1962), II, p. 1.
Newsweek, 60 (15 October 1962), 109.
Motion Picture Herald (17 October 1962), p. 674.
New Yorker, 38 (20 October 1962), 215.
New York Times (22 October 1962), II, p. 7.
Life, 53 (26 October 1962), 70A.
Motion Picture Herald (31 October 1962), p. 21.
Esquire, 58 (December 1962), 22+.
Movie, No. 10 (1963), p. 35.
Monthly Film Bulletin, No. 367 (1964), p. 115.
Kinematograph Weekly (21 May 1964), p. 16.
Daily Cinema (27 May 1964), p. 10.
Sight and Sound, 33 (Summer 1964), p. 147.
Films and Filming (July 1964), p. 20.

89 FAIL SAFE
Filmfacts, VII (1964), 107+.
American Cinematographer, 44 (August 1964), 462-463+.
Hollywood Reporter (11 September 1964), p. 3.
New Republic, 151 (12 September 1964), 26-27.
New York Times (16 September 1964), p. 36.
Variety (16 September 1964).
New York Times (27 September 1964), II, p. 1.

Motion Picture Herald (30 September 1964), p. 138.
Films in Review, XV (October 1964), 506-507.
New York Times (8 October 1964), p. 48.
New Yorker, 40 (10 October 1964), 200-201.
Newsweek, 64 (12 October 1964), 114+.
America, 111 (17 October 1964), 464-465.
Life, 57 (30 October 1964), 12.
National Review, 16 (17 November 1964), 1026-1027.
Monthly Film Bulletin, No. 376 (1965), p. 67.
Daily Cinema (2 April 1965), p. 6.
Kinematograph Weekly (8 April 1965), p. 11.
Films and Filming, 11 (May 1965), 20.
Films and Filming, 11 (June 1965), 21-25.
Sight and Sound, 34 (Spring 1965), 97.
Movie, No. 12 (Spring 1965), p. 45.
Cineforum, No. 52 (February 1966), p. 113.

90 PAWNBROKER
Variety (8 July 1964).
Films and Filming (October 1964), p. 17.
Life, 58 (2 April 1965), 16.
Saturday Review, 48 (3 April 1965), 37.
Film Daily (16 April 1965), p. 3.
Hollywood Reporter (16 April 1965), p. 3.
New York Times (21 April 1965), p. 51.
Time, 85 (23 April 1965), 103+.
New Republic, 152 (24 April 1965), 23.
New Yorker, 41 (24 April 1965), 164-165.
Newsweek, 65 (26 April 1965), 96+.
Motion Picture Herald (28 April 1965), p. 273.
Films in Review, XVI (May 1965), 314-315.
New York Times (2 May 1965), II, p. 1.
Nation, 200 (10 May 1965), 515-516.
Commonweal, 82 (14 May 1965), 255-256.
Film Heritage, 1 (Spring 1966), 3-22.
Daily Cinema (17 October 1966), p. 10.
Kinematograph Weekly (20 October 1966), p. 12.
Films and Filming (December 1966), p. 6.
Monthly Film Bulletin, No. 395 (December 1966), p. 181.
Art et Essai, No. 38 (11 January 1968), p. 6.

91 THE HILL
Monthly Film Bulletin, No. 378 (1965), p. 104.

New York Times (10 January 1965), II, p. 9.
Kinematograph Weekly (27 May 1965), p. 8.
Daily Cinema (28 May 1965), p. 6.
Sight and Sound, 34 (Summer 1965), 148-149.
Variety (9 June 1965).
Films and Filming (August 1965), p. 26.
Saturday Review, 48 (2 October 1965), 30.
New York Times (7 October 1965), Supp., p. 5.
Commonweal, 83 (8 October 1965), 25-26.
New Republic, 153 (9 October 1965), 29-30+.
New Yorker, 41 (9 October 1965), 189-190.
Nation, 201 (25 October 1965), 288.
Newsweek, 66 (25 October 1965), 113-114.
Kinematograph Weekly (29 October 1965), p. 16.
Films in Review, XVI (November 1965), 581-582.
Film Quarterly, XIX (Spring 1966), 52.
Cinema, 4 (Summer 1968), 5-9.

92 THE GROUP

Esquire, 64 (December 1965), 234-237+.
Monthly Film Bulletin, No. 394 (1966), p. 163.
Film Daily (2 March 1966), p. 3.
Variety (2 March 1966).
Hollywood Reporter (11 March 1966), p. 3.
Time, 87 (11 March 1966), 99+.
Motion Picture Herald (16 March 1966), p. 483.
New York Times (17 March 1966), p. 35.
New Yorker, 42 (19 March 1966), 173-174.
Newsweek, 67 (21 March 1966), 105A.
Saturday Review, 49 (26 March 1966), 46.
Films in Review, XVII (April 1966), 250.
Life, 60 (8 April 1966), 116-117.
National Review, 154 (9 April 1966), 480-481.
New Republic, 154 (9 April 1966), 25.
Film Quarterly, XIX (Summer 1966), 59-60.
Cinema, 2 (July 1966), 50.
Films and Filming (September 1966), p. 14.
Daily Cinema (21 September 1966), p. 5.
Kinematograph Weekly (29 September 1966), p. 7.
Sight and Sound, 35 (Autumn 1966), 200.
Cahier du Cinema, No. 197 (January 1968), p. 90.

93 THE DEADLY AFFAIR
New York Times (11 February 1966), p. 36.
New York Times (15 May 1966), II, p. 11.
American Cinematographer, 47 (August 1966), 536-537.
Monthly Film Bulletin, No. 398 (1967), p. 40.
Hollywood Reporter (26 January 1967), p. 3.
Film Daily (27 January 1967), p. 3.
New York Times (27 January 1967), p. 31.
Time, 89 (27 January 1967), 80.
Saturday Review, 50 (28 January 1967), 49.
New York Times (29 January 1967), II, p. 1.
Variety (1 February 1967), p. 6.
Kinematograph Weekly (4 February 1967), p. 9.
New Yorker, 42 (4 February 1967), 98.
Daily Cinema (6 February 1967), p. 8.
Newsweek, 69 (6 February 1967), 97.
Commonweal, 85 (17 February 1967), 566.
Esquire, 67 (March 1967), 20.
Films in Review, XVIII (March 1967), 179-180.
Films and Filming (April 1967), p. 6.
Sight and Sound, 36 (Spring 1967), 96.
Films and Filming (May 1967), p. 37.

94 BYE, BYE BRAVERMAN
New York Times (23 April 1967), II, p. 15.
Hollywood Reporter (2 February 1968), p. 3.
Variety (7 February 1968), p. 6.
Motion Picture Herald (14 February 1968), p. 773.
New York Times (22 February 1968), p. 36.
New Yorker, 44 (2 March 1968), 125.
Saturday Review, 51 (2 March 1968), 40.
Commonweal, 87 (8 March 1968), 87.
New Republic, 158 (9 March 1968), 37.
Nation, 206 (11 March 1968), 356+.
Newsweek, 71 (11 March 1968), 92+.
Time, 91 (15 March 1968), 90+.
Village Voice, 13 (21 March 1968), 47.
Films in Review, XIX (April 1968), 242-243.
Harper's, 236 (May 1968), 92-94.
Sight and Sound, 38 (Autumn 1969), 191-192.

95 THE SEA GULL
Hollywood Reporter (20 December 1968), p. 3.
New York Times (24 December 1968), p. 14.
Variety (25 December 1968), p. 6.
New York Times (29 December 1968), II, p. 29.
Motion Picture Herald (1 January 1969), p. 87.
Today's Cinema (2 January 1969), p. 10.
Time, 93 (3 January 1969), 56.
Village Voice, 14 (9 January 1969), 47-49.
New Republic, 160 (11 January 1969), 20+.
New Yorker, 44 (11 January 1969), 61-65.
New York Times (12 January 1969), II, p. 1.
Newsweek, 73 (13 January 1969), 85.
Saturday Review, 52 (25 January 1969), 22.
Films in Review, XX (February 1969), 117-118.
Sight and Sound, 38 (Autumn 1969), 190-195.
Kinematograph Weekly (27 December 1969), p. 12.
Films and Filming, 16 (February 1970), 39.
Monthly Film Bulletin, No. 433 (February 1970), p. 30.

96 THE APPOINTMENT
Variety (28 May 1969), p. 34.

97 LAST OF THE MOBILE HOT-SHOTS
Hollywood Reporter (22 December 1969), p. 6.
Motion Picture Herald (24 December 1969), p. 348.
Variety (31 December 1969), p. 6.
New York Times (15 January 1970), p. 38.
Time, 95 (19 January 1970), 67.
Film Daily (20 January 1970), p. 4.
Newsweek, 75 (26 January 1970), 75.
Village Voice, 15 (29 January 1970), 51.

98 KING: A FILMED RECORD
New York Times (23 October 1969), p. 47.
Variety (4 March 1970), p. 18.
Hollywood Reporter (12 March 1970), p. 10.
New York Times (15 March 1970), II, p. 15.
Motion Picture Herald (25 March 1970), p. 7.
Films in Review, 21 (April 1970), 245.
Filmmakers Newsletter, 15 (April 1972), 20-23.

99 THE ANDERSON TAPES
   Filmfacts, XIV (1971), 153+.
   Hollywood Reporter (12 May 1971), p. 3.
   Variety (12 May 1971), p. 19.
   Motion Picture Herald (16 June 1971), p. 567.
   New York Times (18 June 1971), p. 23.
   Saturday Review, 54 (10 July 1971), 12.
   Newsweek, 78 (12 July 1971), 82.
   Time, 98 (19 July 1971), 69-70.
   Village Voice, 16 (22 July 1971), 55.
   Commonweal, 94 (6 August 1971), 408.
   Focus on Film, No. 7 (October 1971), p. 7.
   Cineforum, No. 108 (October/November 1971), pp. 65-72.
   Positif, No. 132 (November 1971), pp. 66-67.
   Monthly Film Bulletin, No. 455 (December 1971), p. 235.
   Films and Filming, 18 (March 1972), 57.

100 CHILD'S PLAY
   Hollywood Reporter (5 November 1971), p. 4.
   Filmfacts, XV (1972), 677+.
   New York Times (9 January 1972), II, p. 13.
   Hollywood Reporter (6 December 1972), p. 3.
   Variety (6 December 1972), p. 20.
   Los Angeles (11 December 1972), IV, pp. 1, 27.
   New York Times (13 December 1972), p. 58.
   New Yorker, XLVIII (16 December 1972), 131-132.
   Newsweek, LXXX (18 December 1972), 93-94.
   Time, 100 (18 December 1972), 79.
   New York, 5 (18/25 December 1972), 106, 109.
   Films in Review, XXIV (February 1973), 119-120.
   Commonweal, XCVII (2 February 1973), 398-399.
   St. Louis Post Dispatch (2 March 1973), D, p. 2.
   Cinefantastique, 3 (Fall 1973), 31.
   Cinema TV Today (24 November 1973), p. 52.
   Monthly Film Bulletin, No. 479 (December 1973), p. 246.

101 THE OFFENCE
   Hollywood Reporter (7 April 1972), p. 20.
   Filmfacts, 16 (1973), 146-148.
   Monthly Film Bulletin, No. 468 (January 1973), p. 13.
   Cinema TV Today (20 January 1973), p. 20.

Films and Filming, 19 (March 1973), 57.
New York Times (12 May 1973), p. 19.
Variety (16 May 1973), p. 32.
New York, 6 (28 May 1973), 72-73.
New York Times (3 June 1973), II, p. 11.
Time, 101 (4 June 1973), 97, 99.
Films in Review, XXIV (August/September 1973), 440.
International Film Guide, 11 (1974), 140.

102 SERPICO
Take One, 4 (November/December 1973), 32-33.
Hollywood Reporter (3 December 1973), p. 3.
Variety (5 December 1973), p. 20.
New York Times (6 December 1973), L, p. 61.
New York, 6 (10 December 1973), 93-94.
Los Angeles Times (16 December 1973), Cal., pp. 1, 48-49+.
Nation, 217 (17 December 1973), 667-668.
Newsweek, LXXXII (17 December 1973), 91-92.
New Yorker, XLIX (17 December 1973), 107-110.
New York Times (19 December 1973), p. 58.
Time, 102 (31 December 1973), 51.
Cineaste, VI (1974), 51-52.
New York Times (18 January 1974), p. 66.
New Republic, 170 (19 January 1974), 22.
New York Times (20 January 1974), II, p. 11.
New York Times (21 January 1974), p. 24.
Los Angeles Times (27 January 1974), Cal., pp. 1, 26.
Atlantic, 233 (February 1974), 93-94.
Filmmaker's Newsletter, 7 (February 1974), 30-34.
Films in Review, XXV (February 1974), 119.
Making Films in New York, 8 (February 1974), 6-8.
St. Louis Post Dispatch (15 February 1974), D, p. 5.
Film, 2 (February/March 1974), 16.
Esquire, LXXXI (March 1974), 66, 70.
Harper's, 248 (March 1974), 82-83.
Monthly Film Bulletin, No. 482 (March 1974), pp. 52-53.
Playboy, 21 (March 1974), 30.
Cinema TV Today (6 April 1974), p. 14.
Film Heritage, 9 (Spring 1974), 30.
Focus on Film, No. 17 (Spring 1974), pp. 9-11.

103 LOVIN' MOLLY
Esquire, LXXX (December 1973), 94, 98.

Playboy, 21 (February 1974), 38.
Hollywood Reporter (13 March 1974), p. 3.
Variety (13 March 1974), p. 18.
St. Louis Post Dispatch (22 March 1974), F, p. 5.
Newsweek, LXXXIII (15 April 1974), 101, 103.
New York, 7 (15 April 1974), 79-81.
New York Times (15 April 1974), p. 41.
New Yorker, L (22 April 1974), 136-140.
Time, 103 (22 April 1974), 68, 70.
Los Angeles Times (7 May 1974), IV, p. 28.
Monthly Film Bulletin, No. 496 (May 1975), pp. 110-111.
Screen International (11 October 1975), p. 17.
Films Illustrated, 5 (November 1975), 104.

104 MURDER ON THE ORIENT EXPRESS
Cinema TV Today (26 January 1974), p. 1.
Film, 2 (November 1974), 17.
Variety (20 November 1974), p. 14.
Cinema TV Today (23 November 1974), pp. 16-17.
New York, 7 (25 November 1974), 94.
New York Times (25 November 1974), p. 38.
Film Review, 24 (December 1974), 18.
Films Illustrated, 4 (December 1974), 128-129.
Films in Review, XXV (December 1974), 623-624.
Monthly Film Bulletin, No. 491 (December 1974), pp. 279-280.
Newsweek, LXXXIV (2 December 1974), 107, 111.
New Yorker, L (9 December 1974), 171-172.
Time, 104 (9 December 1974), 4.
Nation, 219 (14 December 1974), 637.
Los Angeles Times (22 December 1974), Cal., pp. 1, 50.
New Republic, 171 (28 December 1974), 20, 34.
Films and Filming, 21 (January 1975), 35-36.
Playboy, 22 (January 1975), 32.
Saturday Review, 2 (11 January 1975), 52.
Commonweal, CI (17 January 1975), 328-330.
Esquire, 83 (February 1975), 36, 44.
St. Louis Post Dispatch (14 February 1975), D, p. 5.
Focus on Film, No. 19 (Autumn 1975), pp. 8-9.

105 DOG DAY AFTERNOON
Variety (27 August 1975), p. 15.
Hollywood Reporter (4 September 1975), pp. 3, 14.
New Yorker, LI (22 September 1975), 95.

New York Times (22 September 1975), L, p. 41.
Newsweek, LXXXVI (29 September 1975), 84.
New York, 8 (29 September 1975), 85.
Playboy, 22 (October 1975), 20-21.
New Republic, 173 (4 October 1975), 20-21.
Saturday Review, 3 (4 October 1975), 35-36.
Los Angeles Times (5 October 1975), Cal., pp. 1, 30.
Time, 106 (6 October 1975), 66, 70.
Nation, 221 (11 October 1975), 347, 349.
Commonweal, CII (24 October 1975), 499.
Films in Review, XXVI (November 1975), 563.
Monthly Film Bulletin, 42 (November 1975), 236-237.
Photoplay Film Monthly, 26 (December 1975), 58-59.
Screen International (13 December 1975), p. 12.
Film Heritage, 11 (Winter 1975-1976), 44-45.
Sight and Sound, 45 (Winter 1975-1976), 57-58.
Films and Filming, 22 (January 1976), 33.
Los Angeles Times (27 January 1976), IV, pp. 1, 10.
Jump Cut, No. 10/11 (10 June 1976), pp. 3-4.
Movie, No. 23 (Winter 1976-1977), pp. 33-36.
New York Times (9 February 1978), III, p. 2.

106 NETWORK
Los Angeles Times (30 May 1976), Cal., pp. 32-34.
Hollywood Reporter (12 October 1976), pp. 3, 21.
Variety (13 October 1976), p. 22.
New York Times (12 November 1976), III, p. 6.
New Republic, 175 (13 November 1976), 22-23.
Saturday Review, 4 (13 November 1976), 44-46.
Los Angeles Times (14 November 1976), Cal., pp. 1, 41-43.
New York Times (15 November 1976), p. 39.
Los Angeles Times (21 November 1976), Cal., pp. 1, 50.
Newsweek, LXXXVIII (22 November 1976), 107.
New York, 9 (22 November 1976), 88, 91-92.
New York Times (28 November 1976), II, p. 17.
Time, 108 (29 November 1976), 79+.
Films in Review, XXVII (December 1976), 635.
Playboy, 23 (December 1976), 34, 36, 40.
Commonweal, CIII (3 December 1976), 784, 786-787.
Nation, 223 (4 December 1976), 605-606.
New Yorker, LII (6 December 1976), 177-185.
Focus on Film, No. 26 (Winter 1976), pp. 11-12.

Monthly Film Bulletin, No. 516 (January 1977), p. 9.
Take One, 5 (January 1977), 41-43.
Screen International (26 February 1977), p. 20.

107 EQUUS
Hollywood Reporter (29 November 1976), p. 18.
Canadian Film Digest (December 1976), pp. 40-41.
New York Times (24 July 1977), II, p. 9.
Films Illustrated, No. 73 (September 1977), pp. 32-33.
Films and Filming, 24 (October 1977), 25-27.
New York Times (5 October 1977), III, p. 17.
Hollywood Reporter (17 October 1977), pp. 3, 9.
New York Times (17 October 1977), p. 39.
Variety (19 October 1977), p. 25.
Films Illustrated, No. 75 (November 1977), p. 86.
Monthly Film Bulletin, No. 526 (November 1977), pp. 232-233.
Screen International (12 November 1977), p. 22.

Distributors of Lumet's Films

108 Alba House
7050 Pinehurst
P.O. Box 35
Dearborn, MI 48126
Long Day's Journey into Night

109 Argosy Film Service
1939 Central Street
Evanston, IL 60201
The Anderson Tapes
Bye, Bye Braverman
Fail Safe

110 Budget Films
4590 Santa Monica Blvd.
Los Angeles, CA 90029
Bye, Bye Braverman
Fail Safe
Long Day's Journey into Night
The Sea Gull

111 Charard Motion Pictures
2110 East 24th Street
Brooklyn, NY 11229
The Deadly Affair
Long Day's Journey into Night

112 Cine-Craft Company
1720 West Marshall
Portland, OR 97209
Bye, Bye Braverman
The Deadly Affair
Fail Safe
Long Day's Journey into Night
The Sea Gull

113 Clem Williams Films
2240 Noblestown Road

Pittsburgh, PA 15205
> *The Deadly Affair*
> *The Sea Gull*

114 Columbia-Warner Distributors
16MM Division
135 Wardour Street
London Wl, England
> *The Anderson Tapes*
> *The Deadly Affair*
> *Dog Day Afternoon*
> *Fail Safe*

115 McGraw-Hill/Contemporary Films
1221 Avenue of the Americas
New York, NY 10020
> *The Deadly Affair*
> *Fail Safe*

116 EMI Film Distributors
16MM Division
142 Wardour Street
London, Wl, England
> *Murder on the Orient Express*

117 The Film Center
908 Twelfth Street, NW
Washington, DC 20005
> *The Anderson Tapes*
> *Bye-Bye Braverman*
> *Long Day's Journey into Night*

118 Film Distributors Association
16MM Ltd.
Building No. 9
GEC Estate
East Lane
Wembley, Middlesex, England
> *The Offence*
> *Twelve Angry Men*

119 Films Incorporated
4420 Oakton Street
Skokie, IL 60076
> *The Appointment*
> *Child's Play*
> *The Hill*
> *Murder on the Orient Express*
> *Serpico*

120 Harris/Films Ltd.
Glenbuck House
Surbiton, Surrey, England
The Hill
Lovin' Molly
The Pawnbroker
Stage Struck

121 Institutional Cinema Service
915 Broadway
New York, NY 10010
The Deadly Affair
Long Day's Journey into Night

122 Ivy Films
165 West 46th Street
New York, NY 10036
Long Day's Journey into Night

123 Kerr Film Exchange
3034 Canon Street
San Diego, CA 92106
Fail Safe
Long Day's Journey into Night

124 Kit Parker Films
P.O. Box 227
Carmel Valley, CA 93924
Fail Safe
Long Day's Journey into Night
The Sea Gull

125 MacMillan Audio-Brandon Films
34 McQuesten Parkway, South
Mount Vernon, NY 10550
The Anderson Tapes
Bye-Bye Braverman
The Deadly Affair
Fail Safe
Long Day's Journey into Night
The Pawnbroker
The Sea Gull

126 Martin Luther King Foundation
154 Balham High Road
London SW 12, England
King: A Filmed Record

127 Modern Sound Pictures

1402 Howard Street
Omaha, NB 68102
> *Bye, Bye Braverman*
> *The Deadly Affair*
> *Fail Safe*
> *Long Day's Journey into Night*
> *The Sea Gull*

128   Mottas Films
1318 Ohio Avenue, NE
Canton, OH 44705
> *Bye, Bye Braverman*
> *The Deadly Affair*
> *Fail Safe*
> *Long Day's Journey into Night*

129   The Movie Center
57 Baldwin Street
Charlestown, MA 02129
> *Long Day's Journey into Night*

130   National Film Service
14 Glenwood Avenue
Raleigh, NC 27602
> *Fail Safe*

131   Newman Film Library
400 32nd Street, SE
Grand Rapids, MI 49508
> *Fail Safe*

132   Rank Film Library
P.O. Box 20
Great West Road
Brentford, Middlesex, England
> *Serpico*
> *That Kind of Woman*

133   ROA's Films
1696 North Astor Street
Milwaukee, WI 53202
> *Bye, Bye Braverman*
> *The Deadly Affair*
> *Fail Safe*
> *Long Day's Journey into Night*
> *The Sea Gull*

134   Select Film Library

115 West 31st Street
New York, NY 10001
> *Bye, Bye Braverman*
> *Fail Safe*
> *Long Day's Journey into Night*

135 Swank Motion Pictures
201 South Jefferson Avenue
St. Louis, MO 63166
> *Bye, Bye Braverman*
> *Dog Day Afternoon*
> *Fail Safe*
> *Lovin' Molly*
> *The Sea Gull*

136 Trans-World Films
322 South Michigan Avenue
Chicago, IL 60604
> *The Sea Gull*

137 Twyman Films
329 Salem Avenue
Dayton, OH 45401
> *Bye, Bye Braverman*
> *The Deadly Affair*
> *Fail Safe*
> *Long Day's Journey into Night*
> *The Sea Gull*

138 United Artists 16
729 Seventh Avenue
New York, NY 10019
> *The Fugitive Kind*
> *The Group*
> *The Offence*
> *Twelve Angry Men*

139 United Films
1425 South Main Street
Tulsa, OK 74119
> *Bye, Bye Braverman*
> *The Deadly Affair*
> *Fail Safe*
> *Long Day's Journey into Night*
> *The Sea Gull*
> *Stage Struck*

140 Walter Reade 16

241 East 34th Street
New York, NY 10016
  A View from the Bridge

141 Warner Brothers
Non-Theatrical Division
4000 Warner Blvd.
Burbank, CA 91505
  Last of the Mobile Hot-Shots

142 Welling Motion Pictures
454 Meacham Avenue
Elmont, NY 11003
  Bye, Bye Braverman
  The Deadly Affair
  Long Day's Journey into Night
  The Sea Gull

143 Westcoast Films
25 Lusk Street
San Francisco, CA 94107
  The Anderson Tapes
  The Deadly Affair
  Fail Safe
  Long Day's Journey into Night
  The Sea Gull

144 Wholesome Film Center
20 Melrose Street
Boston, MA 02116
  The Anderson Tapes
  The Deadly Affair
  Fail Safe
  Long Day's Journey into Night
  The Sea Gull

145 Willoughby-Peerless
110 West 32nd Street
New York, NY 10001
  Bye, Bye Braverman
  Fail Safe
  Long Day's Journey into Night

Title Index

Note: numbers in indices refer to entry numbers rather than pages.

Anderson Tapes, The, 17, 99, 109, 114, 117, 125, 143-144
Appointment, The, 14, 96, 121
Bourgeois Gentleman, The, 72
Brooklyn, U. S. A., 67
Brownville Grandfather, The, 57
Bye, Bye Braverman, 12, 94, 110, 112, 117, 125, 127-128, 133-35, 137, 139, 142, 145
Caligula, 75
Child's Play, 18, 100, 119
Christmas Eve, 64
Dead End, 58
Deadly Affair, The, 11, 38, 93, 111-115, 121, 125, 127-128, 133, 137, 139, 142-144
Doctor's Dilemma, The, 73
Dog Day Afternoon, 23, 105, 114, 135
Equus, 25, 107
Eternal Road, The, 60
Fail Safe, 7, 33, 89, 109-110, 112, 114-115, 123-125, 127-128, 130-131, 133-135, 137, 139, 143-145
Flag Is Born, A, 68
Fugitive Kind, The, 4, 28, 86, 138
Group, The, 10, 41, 92, 138
Hill, The, 9, 42, 91, 119-120
It Can't Happen Here, 59
Journey to Jerusalem, 66, 71
King: A Filmed Record, 15, 98, 126
Last of the Mobile Hot-Shots, 16, 97, 141
Long Day's Journey into Night, 6, 48, 78, 88, 110-112, 117, 121-125, 127-129, 133-134, 137, 139, 142-145
Lovin' Molly, 21, 103, 120, 135
Morning Star, 65
Murder on the Orient Express, 22, 104, 116, 119
My Heart's in the Highlands, 63
Network, 24, 55, 106
Night of the Auk, 74
Nowhere To Go But Up, 76
Offence, The, 19, 49, 101, 118, 138
One Third of a Nation, 70
Pawnbroker, The, 8, 35-37, 80, 90, 120, 125
Schoolhouse on the Lot, 62
Sea Gull, The, 13, 95, 110, 112-113, 124-125, 127, 133, 135-137, 139, 142-144
Seeds in the Wind, 69
Serpico, 20, 52, 102, 119, 132
Stage Struck, 2, 84, 120, 139
Sunup to Sundown, 61
That Kind of Woman, 3, 85, 132
Twelve Angry Men, 1, 83, 118, 138
View from the Bridge, A, 5, 31, 87, 140

149

Name Index

Bean, Robin, 34
Bogdanovich, Peter, 30
Casty, Alan, 35
Cowie, Peter, 44, 54
Farber, Stephen, 47
Flatley, Guy, 51
Foster, Frederick, 28
Gow, Gordon, 53
Grönstedt, Olle, 37
Hirshfield, Gerald, 33
Hultman, Bo Johan, 37
Kael, Pauline, 41
Kerner, Bruce, 42
Labarca, Daniel, 46
Luciano, Dale, 48
Lumet, Sidney, 77•82
Manns, Torsten, 37
Merrill, Susan, 49
Moskowitz, Gene, 27
Petrie, Graham, 40
Roizman, Owen, 55
Sarris, Andrew, 45
Sharples, Win, Jr., 52
Steele, Robert, 36
Young, Freddie, 38